AF269917

# MY NOTHING IS SOMEONE ELSE'S EVERYTHING

# MY NOTHING IS SOMEONE ELSE'S

**DR. BARB REMBIESA, D.Litt**

FOREWORD by ANDY ANDREWS, *NEW YORK TIMES* BESTSELLING AUTHOR
and CEO of CREATINGMEASURABLERESULTS.COM

*My Nothing Is Someone Else's Everything:*
*How Small Acts Can Create Big Change*


Published by Forefront Books, Nashville, Tennessee.
Distributed by Simon & Schuster.

Library of Congress Control Number: 2026905642

Print ISBN: 978-1-63763-560-5
E-book ISBN: 978-1-63763-561-2

Cover Design by Mary Susan Oleson, Blu Design Concepts
Interior Design by Mary Susan Oleson, Blu Design Concepts

Printed in the United States of America

26 27 28 29 30 31 RR4 10 9 8 7 6 5 4 3 2 1

*To those who feel the desire to give but aren't sure where to begin, my hope is that this book ignites something inside you. May it help you see the beautiful ways God can work through even the smallest act of kindness.*

*And to those who believe they "do nothing," I pray these words open your eyes to the truth: God often uses the simple, ordinary moments, the ones you overlook, to become someone else's blessing. Your nothing may be the very thing He uses as someone else's everything.*

*—Dr. Barb*

# Contents

*Section Two: Time Nothings*



*Section Three: Networking Nothings*

# *Foreword*

FROM THE VERY beginning—when I met her at the first IAITAM conference—I knew Dr. Barb Rembiesa was someone special. This was before she became such a massive influence in my life and in the lives of my wife and our two sons. I often boast to businesspeople that I knew Dr. Barb before her name became synonymous with integrity, leadership, and boundless energy.

Even then, she radiated a distinct purpose that drew people happily into her orbit. Over the years, I've watched her spark grow into a movement that has changed lives around the world. I've also been privileged to share in many of her personal milestones—including having the honor of performing the wedding ceremony for Barb and her amazing husband, Dave.

In this book—the first of what I hope will be many more—Dr. Barb takes us beyond the boardroom and into the heart of what really matters. *My Nothing Is Someone*

*Else's Everything* proves that kindness isn't measured by its size but by its sincerity and impact. The smallest, most intentional acts—the ones we might dismiss as nothing—often land in someone else's life as everything.

Over the years, I've watched Dr. Barb transform lives and situations—ones most folks would have never taken a second look at. She has not only rescued people and shaped careers, but incredibly, she single-handedly created an entire industry. (Check out the member/client list on IAITAM.com sometime.) Still, if you ask her, Barb will tell you her greatest success stories continue to begin in moments no one else even notices.

The stories in this book reveal a truth that transcends business, culture, and circumstance: Greatness begins in the ordinary. Whether it's a word of encouragement, a simple favor, or a moment of understanding, each gesture carries the power to transform a day, a career, or even a lifetime.

I am witness to the fact that Dr. Barb doesn't just teach this principle—she lives it. She has quietly modeled compassion and courage for decades, proving that leadership, at its best, is really love in action.

So take a deep breath, turn the page, and prepare

to see the world a little differently—because after reading this book, you'll never again underestimate the impact of a single, intentional act of kindness.

— *Andy Andrews*
*New York Times* bestselling author and CEO
of CreatingMeasurableResults.com

# *Preface*

I BELIEVE WITH all my heart that God gives each of us everything we need to make a difference in this world. But here's the paradox: Sometimes that "everything" feels like "nothing".

Let me explain.

Each of us has been given unique talents, experiences, and strengths. For some, writing a heartfelt note comes naturally. For others, it feels like an impossible task. Some of us effortlessly connect people in our network, while others struggle to even ask for help. You might have a knack for organizing, fixing things, or simply listening, and think, *That's just who I am.* But what you view as easy, ordinary, or insignificant—your "nothing"—could be someone else's everything.

It's in this realization that this book was born.

I've seen how the smallest gesture, smile, phone call, kind word, or warm meal can transform another person's day—or even their entire life. What takes very little effort from one individual could be just the thing to bring hope, healing, or relief to another. When we share what comes easily to us—the things that don't cost much but come from the heart—we are actually giving our "nothing," and in doing so, we may be answering someone else's prayer.

In these pages, I explore what I call "nothings" in three areas: **Finances**, **Time**, and **Networking**. Each section is filled with real-life stories, practical suggestions, and encouraging reflections that show how everyday actions can create extraordinary impact. This isn't about performing grand gestures or making major sacrifices. It's about slowing down, tuning in, and listening to that quiet voice inside that nudges us to act, being intentional with what we already have.

In a world where so much emphasis is placed on what we can *earn*, I challenge you to focus on what you can *give*. It doesn't need to cost money. It doesn't need to be complicated. But it does need to come from a place of genuine care.

I truly believe that when we begin living with the mindset of offering our "nothing" each day, whether it's a few minutes of encouragement, a small financial gift, a connection between two people, or simply being present, we unlock the deeper purpose God has planted within us. And the beauty is, we don't need to have it all together. We just need to be willing.

As you read this book, I hope you'll begin to recognize your own "nothings"—the gifts that come easily to you, the things you've overlooked, the quiet nudges you've ignored. And more importantly, I hope you begin to share them. Because what you think is small might just be the "everything" someone else is waiting for.

And always remember this: *God doesn't make junk.* He created each of us with intention and purpose. He gave you something special, not to keep for yourself but to lift others up. Don't let the world convince you that your gifts need to be big and flashy to matter. The world doesn't need more noise—it needs more *intentional love.*

May you discover your "nothing" within these pages, and may it become someone else's "everything."

With gratitude and purpose,

*Dr. Barb Rembiesa*

INTRODUCTION

# *My "Nothing" Is Someone Else's "Everything"*

THE SUNLIGHT STREAMED through my office window, casting long, golden rays across my desk. I leaned back in my chair, enjoying the cool blast from the AC, a stark contrast to the warm day outside. The usual hum of voices and the tapping of keyboards filled the office when suddenly, a conversation caught my attention. Some of my coworkers were talking about Lotts Creek, a remote community in Kentucky, home to the last settlement school in the United States. From what they were saying, it sounded like the school's situation was dire—no technology and minimal resources for struggling families who were trying to educate their children with limited means.

I couldn't ignore it. I turned in my chair and asked a simple question: "Does the school have any technology at all?" The answer was a resounding no. That was all I needed to hear. With a few quick phone calls to my network, the wheels were set in motion. Help began to pour in from unexpected places. Soon, three massive twenty-four-foot trucks, each one packed to the brim with computers, food bank supplies, and other essentials, were making their way from Ohio to Lotts Creek, Kentucky.

One story from this situation still stands out vividly in my mind. A promising high school athlete, who was just one online course away from securing a full-ride college basketball scholarship, was at risk of losing everything. Without the necessary technology, he couldn't complete his last required class. But with the resources we provided, he was able to finish the course and secure his scholarship.

To me, it felt like such a small effort—just making a few calls and connecting the right people—but to him, it was life-changing. I have always been a giver, but this was the moment that cemented my understanding: What we often perceive as nothing can, in fact, be everything for someone else.

Years later, during the COVID-19 pandemic, I received a heartfelt message from the Lotts Creek community. The technology we had sent them was now a lifeline, allowing parents to work remotely and keep their families afloat. When people asked what I had done to help, I always downplayed it: "Oh, I just made a few calls." But what I learned was that our small, effortless acts—our "nothing"—can be the very thing that transforms lives.

Every single one of us possesses something unique. Some have wealth, others have time, knowledge, or connections. But in our day-to-day lives, we often focus on what we *don't* have. We look at the gaps, the missing pieces, the resources we *wish* we had. But the truth is, what seems insignificant to us might very well be the missing piece for someone else—and it could change their life.

## SHIFTING OUR PERSPECTIVE

Have you ever brushed off something you did as "no big deal"? Maybe you offered much-needed advice, introduced someone to a key connection, or gave a few extra dollars as a tip. These acts might feel minor, but to the recipient, they could be monumental.

Let's take a minute to reflect on some questions:

- Do you have more time than money, or more money than time?
- Do you have knowledge or skills that others could benefit from?
- Are you well-connected in your industry or community?

By identifying your seemingly small assets, you can begin to see the value in what you already have. Your "nothing"—whether it's time, expertise, or encouragement—can be everything to someone in need.

## THE RIPPLE EFFECT OF "NOTHING"

A single act of kindness can set off a chain reaction of good. History is full of examples of people who made an extraordinary impact by simply starting with what seemed like nothing.

Consider Mother Teresa: She had no money when she began her mission, just an unyielding calling to serve. Yet her work inspired millions to contribute in their own ways. Likewise, everyday individuals who commit small acts of generosity often create ripple effects far beyond what they ever imagined.

A kind word, a listening ear, an unexpected gesture—these actions, however small, have the power to shape the world around us. But recognizing and acting on "nothing" opportunities requires awareness. It's about seeing the world differently, noticing the unnoticed, and tuning in to the moments that might otherwise pass us by.

## A STORY OF "NOTHING"

One sunlit summer afternoon, I found myself sitting outside at a high-top table, soaking in the warmth of the day. The air was filled with the sound of chatter and clinking glasses. Then along came Sally, my server for the afternoon. She radiated warmth, her bright smile making me feel instantly at home.

As Sally took my order, she struck up a conversation with me, asking where I was from, what I did, and whether I had experienced the local culture yet. Her enthusiasm was infectious. Then she leaned in slightly, her voice taking on a conspiratorial tone. "You have to try the buffalo blue oysters. They're the best on the menu," she said with a twinkle in her eye. Her excitement was enough to convince me to change my order on the spot.

Minutes later, she returned with a sizzling-hot cast-iron pan. The aroma was intoxicating—buffalo sauce mingled with melted blue cheese bubbling on top of perfectly cooked oysters. It was, hands down, one of the best things I've ever tasted.

As we chatted further, Sally revealed she was working multiple jobs while putting herself through school. She never asked for help, never hinted at needing anything, but because I was *listening*, I recognized an opportunity. I left her an extra-large tip and offered to introduce her to someone in her field of study.

For me, it was just a simple moment. But for Sally, it was more than that. Someone had noticed her hard work, taken note of her passion, and listened to her dreams. The monetary tip and the professional connection I was able to provide? It may have seemed like nothing to me, but it was everything to her.

## THREE TYPES OF "NOTHINGS"

Opportunities to make a difference exist all around us. The more we tune in to these moments, the more obvious they become. Once we start recognizing them, we'll wonder how we ever overlooked them before. Acts of kindness, no matter how small, can change the trajectory of someone's day—or even their life.

Now let's talk a bit more about the three types of "nothings" that have the power to create meaningful change.

*Financial "Nothings"*

Money is often seen as the most tangible way to give, but not all financial contributions need to be large to make an impact. A seemingly small gesture—covering someone's coffee order, donating a bag of groceries to a struggling family, contributing to a scholarship fund—can mean everything to someone in need. It's not about the amount; it's about the intention and the impact it creates.

Financial "nothings" can also take the form of indirect support. Perhaps you know of a local business that's in need of more customers, so you spread the word about them or make a purchase. Maybe you see a server working tirelessly, so you leave a more generous tip than usual. Or you quietly cover the cost of someone's coffee, groceries, or parking fee—never asking for recognition, simply choosing to ease a small burden. These moments of financial generosity, however small, can make someone feel seen, appreciated, and valued.

*Time "Nothings"*

Time is one of our most precious resources, yet giving even a little of it can have profound effects. We often get caught up in our own busy schedules and fail to notice that just a few minutes or hours out of our day could make all the difference to someone else.

Giving your time can mean volunteering at a local charity, mentoring someone who is struggling to navigate their career, or simply being present and listening when another person needs to talk. It could be something as easy as helping a neighbor carry their groceries from their car to their house or spending an hour or two with someone who is feeling lonely.

Unlike financial giving, which may require money you might not always have, giving your time is about prioritizing. When you intentionally open up your schedule to make time for someone else, you send the message that they matter.

*Networking "Nothings"*

Many people underestimate the power of connection. The right introduction, a shared contact, or a word of advice from someone with relevant experience can open doors that otherwise would have remained closed.

Networking "nothings" can be as simple as introducing a job seeker to someone who is hiring, recommending a friend's business to an individual or company who could use their services, or forwarding someone in your circle an opportunity that seems perfect for them.

You may not think twice about sending a quick email or making an introduction, but for the recipient, it could be a game-changer. Sometimes, succeeding isn't about working harder; it's about knowing the right people, and you might be the bridge that helps someone get to where they need to go.

Each of these "nothings"—whether financial, time-based, or networking—can make a significant difference in a person's life. When you train yourself to recognize these opportunities, you begin to see the world in a new light. Small actions, done consistently, can create waves of positive change. And opportunities to do "nothing" exist in every corner of our daily lives:

- **Offering advice** to someone who's unsure of their next steps
- **Leaving an extra tip** to acknowledge an individual's hard work

- **Connecting two people** who might benefit from knowing each other
- **Listening** to someone who needs to be heard

These acts don't require great wealth, influence, or meticulous planning. They only require us to be present, to care, and to act.

## THE CHALLENGE: ONE "NOTHING" A DAY

Every day, I challenge myself to find at least one "nothing" opportunity. The more I practice, the easier it becomes. And the more I recognize these moments, the more I see their impact. I challenge you to try it too. Here are a few ideas to get you started:

- Offer guidance to someone who's unsure of their path.
- Make an introduction that changes a person's career trajectory.
- Speak a kind word or give a genuine compliment.

As we continue to seek out these "nothing" opportunities, let's broaden our collective impact. By sharing our experiences, inspiring others, and fostering a culture of generosity, we can create a world where kindness is instinctive.

Every act of giving, no matter how small, carries immense power. And in the end, we'll come to realize that our "nothing" was never really nothing at all—it was *everything.*

SECTION ONE

# FINANCIAL NOTHINGS

# *When Nothing Becomes Everything*

When we think about helping others, financial contributions are often the first thing that comes to mind. Money may seem like a finite resource, and many of us feel like we don't have enough of it to make a meaningful difference in another person's life. Yet even the smallest financial gesture can ripple outward and make a profound impact. For so many people in our world—a retiree on a fixed income struggling to keep the lights on, a student striving to afford tuition, a military family navigating the challenges of deployment—any type of financial assistance would ease their burdens.

Picture a single parent working tirelessly to provide for their children, only to fall short on grocery money at the end of the month. A modest donation to a local food pantry—perhaps an amount so small that the donor hardly notices it—can help put nourishing meals on the table. To the donor, the act might feel insignificant. But to the family receiving that aid, it represents sustenance, stability, and hope during a difficult time.

Financial "nothings" extend beyond giving direct aid to supporting the broader fabric of community life. Contributions to local arts programs, for example, might not seem urgent compared to other pressing needs, yet these programs offer emotional and creative outlets for individuals of all ages. Similarly, disaster relief funds rely on many small contributions that quickly add up to rebuild lives after hurricanes, wildfires, or earthquakes. These cumulative efforts, born from countless individuals giving what they perceive to be nothing, don't just help people survive—they help communities thrive.

In the service industry, a simple act of financial generosity can transform someone's day. A generous tip to a struggling server, a grocery store gift card for a neighbor in need—these gestures, though seemingly small, can bridge the gap between hardship and relief. Sometimes it's quietly paying for the car behind you in a drive-through or slipping a few extra dollars into a donation jar without any explanation. Actions like these serve as a reminder that financial contributions don't have to be grandiose to be meaningful. The true power of giving lies not in the size of the gift but in the intention behind it and the impact it creates.

Education is another powerful avenue for financial giving. Even a modest scholarship can alleviate tuition stress and allow a student to focus on their studies. Imagine the bright minds and potential world-changers who are held back simply due to financial barriers. A seemingly small contribution could alter the course of a student's life, empowering them to achieve their dreams and ultimately contribute to society in meaningful ways.

For military families, financial support carries profound significance. These families often endure unique hardships, frequent relocations, long separations, and the emotional toll of service. Helping them navigate financial challenges is not just an act of generosity; it's a way of honoring their sacrifice and ensuring they receive the stability they deserve.

Beyond individual assistance, financial giving plays a crucial role in addressing systemic challenges. Contributions to organizations that combat poverty, promote education, or protect the environment help lay the foundation for long-term solutions. Though a single donation may feel like a drop in the ocean, it becomes part of a much larger wave of change. When people unite their resources, even the smallest financial "nothing" can accumulate into transformative impact.

Consider the ripple effect that occurs when one person chooses to give. A single act of generosity can inspire others to pay it forward, creating a chain of goodwill that touches countless lives. History is rich with stories of individuals who started with what seemed like nothing, only to create extraordinary change.

The concept of "nothing" is deeply personal, shaped by our own experiences, limitations, and perceptions of worth. However, when we shift our mindset from comparison to contribution, we unlock the potential within our unique resources. The opportunities to give surround us—and sometimes we find them in the most unexpected ways.

Imagine the quiet, everyday moments when you have the chance to offer what you have, not out of abundance, but out of awareness. It might be adding a few extra dollars to a tip, making a small purchase for the person in line ahead of you, or handing a gift card to a neighbor who's quietly struggling. These financial "nothings" may seem small to the giver, but to the person receiving them, they can bring real relief and a sense of dignity. And often, they're paired with something just as meaningful: a smile, a kind word, a simple acknowledgment that says, "I see you." In a hurried, disconnected world, pausing to offer even a small act of financial kindness becomes a powerful reminder that no one walks alone.

Consider a small town that rallies around a struggling family. Some donate money, others provide home-cooked meals, and a few volunteer their time to help with childcare and repairs. Alone, each contribution might seem minor. But together, they lift the family from despair to stability. There's power in collective giving, and all of us have something we can offer.

The beauty of sharing our "nothing" is that it often leads to unexpected rewards. When we give freely, without expectation, we cultivate a spirit of connection and mutual support. These acts of generosity strengthen relationships, build trust, and foster a sense of belonging. They remind us that we are all interconnected and that even the smallest contribution can have an immeasurable impact.

It's also vital to acknowledge that giving isn't always

an outward act, directed at someone else. Sometimes, sharing our "nothing" means investing in our own growth and well-being. When we take care of ourselves—learning a new skill, seeking mentorship, or simply practicing self-care—we become better equipped to uplift others. By nurturing our own potential, we expand our ability to contribute to the world around us.

To begin exploring how what we think of as nothing can become everything, we'll start with financial resources. This section invites you to look closely at the small, everyday financial choices already within your reach—those quiet moments when a little generosity can ease a burden, restore dignity, and offer hope. As you'll see, even the smallest financial gestures can create ripples that extend far beyond the moment, reminding us that meaningful impact doesn't require abundance, only awareness and intention.

## CHAPTER 1

# *Small Donations*

EMMA WAS SCROLLING through her social media feed when she came across a crowdfunding campaign for the library in her town. The library had been a cornerstone of the community for decades, offering free access to books, computers, and educational programs, but it was now in danger of closing due to budget cuts. The campaign wasn't asking for large donations, just small contributions to help keep the doors open for another year.

Emma didn't think much of her ten-dollar donation at first. She actually felt a pang of guilt when she made it, wondering if such a small amount could really make a difference. But the next week, she received an update from the campaign organizer. The collective effort of hundreds of small donations had surpassed the goal, and the library's future was secure. Her ten dollars, combined with the contributions of others, had played a part in preserving an invaluable resource for the community.

A few months later, Emma attended a storytime event at the library with her niece. As she watched the children laughing with friends and engaging with books, she realized the true impact of her donation. Her small contribution had helped preserve a space where little ones could learn, families could connect, and the community could thrive. It was a powerful reminder that even small acts of generosity ripple outward and create lasting change.

## THE POWER OF SMALL DONATIONS

Small donations often go overlooked, but their impact can be extraordinary when they're combined with the efforts of others. Crowdfunding campaigns, local charities, and community projects rely on these contributions to create meaningful change. By giving what you can, you're not just providing financial support; you're showing solidarity with and belief in a cause.

## PRACTICAL WAYS TO MAKE SMALL DONATIONS

- **Round-Up Programs:** Many apps and stores offer the option to round up your purchase total to the nearest dollar and donate the difference to charity.
- **Crowdfunding Platforms:** Support initiatives on platforms like GoFundMe or Kickstarter, especially those tied to local projects or personal causes.
- **Recurring Microdonations:** Set up small monthly donations to a charity or nonprofit that aligns with your values.
- **Community Events:** Donate to bake sales, car washes, or other small fundraisers organized by schools or local groups.
- **Charity Drives:** Contribute to seasonal donation drives for food bank items, holiday gifts, or school supplies.

Small donations demonstrate that you don't need to give large amounts to make a difference. When combined with the efforts of a community, even the most modest contributions can lead to transformative outcomes.

## THE RIPPLE EFFECT OF SMALL DONATIONS

Emma's ten-dollar gift didn't just help save a library; it preserved a place where children learn, neighbors connect, and hope is renewed. Her small act joined hundreds of others to create something powerful: community change.

That's the beauty of small donations. An individual act of giving may seem insignificant, but when combined with other donations, they can build bridges, feed families, and open doors of opportunity. Each gift, no matter the size, sends a message that generosity isn't about how much we give—it's that we choose to give at all. When we offer what we can, our small "nothings" join with others, to become something extraordinary, rippling outward in ways that make a big difference.

CHAPTER 2

# *Spontaneous Generosity*

MICHAEL WORKED AS a barista at a small café in a bustling city. One chilly morning, as the café filled with the usual rush of commuters and regulars, a young woman named Emily came up to the counter. She looked exhausted, clutching a worn backpack and hesitating as she counted out change for a cup of coffee. Before she could pay, the man in line behind her stepped forward and handed Michael a twenty-dollar bill. "This is to cover her coffee and anything else she might need," the man said quietly. He smiled at Emily, who looked surprised and grateful, and then walked away without another word.

Emily ordered a latte and a sandwich, thanking Michael profusely. Later that day, she returned to the café and explained that she had just moved to the city for a new job and had been overwhelmed by the challenges of finding her footing. That small act of kindness restored her faith and gave her the boost she needed to keep going. And Emily never forgot the stranger's gesture. Inspired by his kindness, she began paying for someone else's meal or coffee whenever she could afford it, hoping to pass along the generosity that had made such an impact on her.

## THE POWER OF SPONTANEOUS GENEROSITY

Covering the cost of someone else's meal or coffee might seem like a small gesture, but it carries a profound message: Someone cares. For the recipient, it can serve as a much-needed moment of hope and a reminder of the goodness that exists in the world. For the giver, it's an opportunity to spread kindness and inspire others to do the same.

## PRACTICAL WAYS TO PRACTICE SPONTANEOUS GENEROSITY

- **Pay at the Register:** Let the cashier know you'd like to pay for the next customer's order.

- **Leave a Note:** Attach a kind message when covering a meal or coffee, making the gesture even more personal.
- **Participate in Pay-It-Forward Chains:** Many cafés and restaurants have programs where customers can pay in advance for someone else's order.
- **Help During the Holidays:** Cover a family's meal during festive seasons or contribute to programs that provide holiday dinners for those in need.
- **Support Local Restaurants:** Partner with small businesses to anonymously purchase meals for customers who are facing financial hardship.

## THE RIPPLE EFFECT OF SPONTANEOUS GENEROSITY

The man who quietly paid for Emily's coffee never knew how far his kindness would travel. His single act didn't end at the counter; it lived on in every cup of coffee or meal Emily later paid forward, in every stranger who felt seen, and in every heart that was reminded that goodness still exists in this world. That's the beauty of anonymous generosity: It plants seeds of kindness that grow unseen but bear visible fruit. One simple gesture can spark a chain reaction of compassion, spreading hope to countless lives. When we give without expecting recognition, we remind the world that love doesn't need an audience—it simply needs action.

CHAPTER 3

# *Gift Cards*

Rachel had a collection of gift cards accumulating in her wallet. Some were for stores she rarely visited, while others had small balances left on them. She often forgot the cards were there, dismissing them as too insignificant to bother using. One day, while volunteering at a local shelter, Rachel met a single mother, Maria, who was trying to rebuild her life after escaping an abusive relationship. Maria shared how difficult it had been to provide basic necessities for her two young children while she was searching for stable employment.

Moved by Maria's story, Rachel decided to gather her unused gift cards—including a card for a department store, another for a chain grocery store, and one for a local coffee shop—and donate them to her new friend at the shelter. When Rachel handed the gift cards to Maria, she was met with tears of gratitude.

Maria used the grocery gift card to stock her kitchen with healthy food and the department store gift card to buy new clothes for her children. She used the coffee shop gift card to purchase small treats for herself and the kids after a long day. For Rachel, handing Maria the gift cards that had been taking up space in her wallet was a simple gesture. But for Maria, it was a lifeline that offered comfort and relief during a challenging time.

## THE POWER OF GIFT CARDS

Gift cards are an easy and impactful way to help others. By donating cards that might otherwise go unused, you turn your "nothing" into a source of hope and opportunity for someone else.

Whether they're fully loaded or partially used, gift cards are more than just pieces of plastic. They represent access—to food, clothing, experiences, and small moments of normalcy that can mean the world to someone in need. What might seem like an insignificant amount to one person can provide critical support and a sense of dignity to another.

## PRACTICAL WAYS TO DONATE GIFT CARDS

- **Local Shelters:** Donate cards for grocery stores, clothing retailers, or big-box stores to shelters that support individuals and families.
- **Schools:** Provide gift cards to teachers or school counselors, who can distribute them to students in need.
- **Community Organizations:** Partner with nonprofits that serve specific groups, such as veterans, refugees, or single parents.
- **Mail-in Programs:** Some organizations accept gift cards by mail to redistribute to those in need.
- **Pay It Forward:** Hand a gift card directly to someone you see struggling, offering immediate assistance without strings attached.

## THE RIPPLE EFFECT OF GIFT CARDS

Rachel's small stack of forgotten gift cards became the bridge between one woman's struggle and her new beginning. What had once sat unused in a wallet turned into meals shared, children clothed, and moments of peace restored. And that simple act of giving didn't stop with Maria. Inspired by Rachel's generosity, others working at the shelter began donating their own unused gift cards, creating a chain of compassion that reached dozens of families.

This is the quiet power of giving what seems like nothing. A few leftover dollars on one person's gift card can become the spark that lights hope in someone else's darkest season. When we release what we no longer need, God multiplies it, turning ordinary things into extraordinary blessings that ripple far beyond what we can see.

## CHAPTER 4

# *School Supplies*

Mia was a third-grade teacher in a rural school district where many families struggled to afford basic necessities, let alone school supplies. Every year, she noticed some of her students came to class without notebooks, pencils, or backpacks. Mia did her best to share her own resources, but the need always seemed greater than what she alone could provide.

One summer, a local community member, Ethan, decided to make a difference. He had heard about the challenges in the district and decided to organize a school supply drive. Ethan reached out to local businesses and friends and posted on social media to spread the word. Soon, donations began pouring in—crayons, binders, backpacks, and more.

When the new school year started, Ethan delivered the supplies to Mia's school. The look of joy on the students' faces was unforgettable. They each received their own set of brand-new school supplies, and for the first time, many of them felt prepared for class and excited to learn. One student, Leah, shyly approached Mia after class and said, "I've never had my own set of markers before. Thank you." That moment showed Mia the profound impact a small act of kindness can have.

Ethan's initiative not only provided much-needed resources for students in need but also inspired others in the community to get involved. The school supply drive became an annual tradition, ensuring that every student in the district started their year on the right foot with a brand-new set of school supplies.

## THE POWER OF SCHOOL SUPPLIES

School supplies are more than just tools for learning—they're symbols of hope, opportunity, and equality. You can contact a teacher to ask about purchasing supplies for individual students, or you can organize a community donation drive for schools in underserved areas. When students have the basic materials they need, they feel more confident, capable, and included. A small donation of school supplies can empower a child to engage fully in their education, fostering a lifelong love of learning.

## PRACTICAL WAYS TO DONATE SCHOOL SUPPLIES

- **Back-to-School Drives:** Participate in or organize school supply drives in your community or workplace.
- **Adopt a Classroom:** Work with teachers to identify and provide the specific supplies their students need.
- **Partner with Nonprofits:** Donate to organizations like Kids In Need Foundation, which distributes supplies to underserved schools.
- **Shop Sales:** Purchase discounted items during back-to-school sales and donate them to local schools or charities.
- **Direct Contributions:** Provide supplies directly to families or students you know may be struggling.
- **Gift Cards for Teachers:** Give teachers gift cards to stores where they can purchase classroom essentials.

- **Create Supply Kits:** Assemble kits with essentials like pencils, notebooks, rulers, and erasers for distribution.

## THE RIPPLE EFFECT OF SCHOOL SUPPLIES

Ethan's simple idea to collect school supplies did more than fill backpacks—it filled hearts with hope. Each notebook and pencil became a reminder to the students that someone believed in them. That belief sparked confidence, which blossomed into participation, learning, and pride.

The drive wasn't just limited to a single school year; it became a community tradition. Parents volunteered, businesses donated, and students who'd once received supplies began helping to distribute them. One small act of generosity grew into a movement that transformed the spirit of an entire district.

When we invest in a child's education, even with something as small as a new pack of pencils, we plant seeds of opportunity that can grow for generations. The ripple begins with one giver but continues through every child who learns, dreams, and dares to reach a little higher.

## CHAPTER 5

# *Clothing Donations*

DURING THE HARSH winter months, Megan often noticed children walking to school without warm jackets or suitable shoes. One day, she passed a young boy, Alex, who was shivering at the bus stop, wearing only a thin hoodie and sneakers with holes. The image stayed with her all day, and she couldn't shake the feeling that she needed to do something.

That evening, Megan went through her closet and found several winter coats her own children had outgrown. She then reached out to her local theater group, sharing Alex's story and asking for donations of warm clothing. The response was overwhelming, and within days, her porch was filled with bags of jackets, scarves, gloves, and boots.

Megan contacted the head counselor at her children's school, who discreetly distributed the clothing to students in need, including Alex. When Megan later saw Alex bundled up in a warm coat, smiling as he played in the snow, she felt a deep sense of gratitude. What had started as a simple observation had turned into a collective act of kindness that warmed not only the children's bodies but also their hearts.

## THE POWER OF CLOTHING DONATIONS

Clothing is a basic necessity, yet many individuals and families struggle to afford appropriate attire for the weather or specific occasions, such as job interviews or school events. Donating clothes is about more than keeping someone warm; it's about restoring dignity and providing comfort during challenging times. A warm coat can mean the difference between a child staying home on a cold day or making it safely to school, ready to learn.

## PRACTICAL WAYS TO DONATE CLOTHING

- **Seasonal Drives:** Organize or participate in winter coat drives, sock collections, or back-to-school clothing initiatives.

- **Partner with Shelters:** Donate essentials like socks, underwear, and coats to local homeless or domestic violence shelters.
- **Support Job Seekers:** Provide gently used professional attire to organizations that help individuals prepare for job interviews.
- **School Donations:** Work with schools to identify students who are in need of uniforms, jackets, or shoes.
- **Thrift Store Contributions:** Donate to secondhand stores that use their proceeds to support community programs.
- **Specialty Needs:** Offer maternity wear, adaptive clothing for people with disabilities, or athletic gear to groups serving specific populations.
- **Community Networks:** Use neighborhood-based online groups to connect directly with families in need, responding to specific requests, such as children's clothing by size or seasonal essentials. This makes your help practical, timely, and personal.

## THE RIPPLE EFFECT OF CLOTHING DONATIONS

When you donate clothing, you're doing more than just clearing out your closet or going shopping—you're giving someone a chance to feel comfortable, confident, and cared for. Megan's story highlights how one small act of compassion can inspire a community to come together and make a difference. Whether it's a pair of thick socks or a winter coat, your contribution can bring warmth and hope to someone in need.

## CHAPTER 6

# *Community Funds*

In the center of the neighborhood sat a vacant lot, overgrown with weeds and littered with debris. For years, it was an eyesore that residents simply avoided. But one day, Sarah, a local mother of two, looked at the lot with a different vision. She imagined a playground where children could laugh, play, and build friendships.

Sarah shared her idea with a few neighbors, and they, too, saw the potential. Together, they decided to raise funds to transform the neglected lot into a vibrant community space. They started small, pooling their own resources and organizing bake sales, car washes, and a neighborhood garage sale. Sarah also created an online crowdfunding campaign, sharing the vision with people outside the neighborhood. The response was overwhelming. Donations began pouring in from former residents, local businesses, and even strangers who were inspired by the project. Within months, they had raised enough money to purchase playground equipment, benches, and landscaping materials.

On the day of the playground's grand opening, the entire community gathered to celebrate. Children raced to the swings and slides, while parents enjoyed the sense of camaraderie the new space brought. The playground became a hub for events like movie nights, picnics, and holiday celebrations. What was once a sketchy, abandoned lot had become the heart of the neighborhood, a place where relationships flourished, memories were made, and the community grew stronger.

## THE POWER OF COMMUNITY FUNDS

Community funds are powerful tools for change. By pooling resources, neighbors can achieve goals that benefit everyone, from building infrastructure like playgrounds to organizing cultural events. These initiatives foster a sense of ownership and pride, creating stronger, more connected communities. Even small contributions can add up to significant results, proving that collective efforts have extraordinary potential.

## PRACTICAL WAYS TO RAISE COMMUNITY FUNDS

- **Crowdfunding Platforms:** Start or contribute to online campaigns for projects like park renovations, community gardens, or local art installations.
- **Neighborhood Associations:** Join homeowner or neighborhood associations that pool resources for shared goals.
- **Local Events:** Support fundraisers like bake sales, car washes, or silent auctions organized by community groups.
- **Sponsor Initiatives:** Partner with local businesses to raise funds for playground equipment, sports leagues, or holiday events.
- **Volunteer Your Skills:** Offer your expertise, such as grant writing, event planning, or construction, to reduce project costs.
- **School Partnerships:** Contribute to initiatives like creating safe play spaces or upgrading library facilities in local schools.

- **Advocate for Matching Funds:** Encourage local government organizations or businesses to match community-raised funds to amplify impact.

## THE RIPPLE EFFECT OF COMMUNITY FUNDS

Sarah's story demonstrates how a simple idea, fueled by collective support, can transform not just a physical space but also the spirit of a community. The playground became more than a place to play—it was a symbol of what people could accomplish when they came together with a shared purpose.

By contributing to community funds, you're investing in more than a project. You're helping to build connections, foster pride, and create spaces where individuals and families can thrive. Whether it's a playground, a garden, or an annual celebration, these initiatives remind us of the incredible power of working together to transform an area and make a difference.

CHAPTER 7

# *Emergency Aid*

One summer evening, Lisa's car broke down on the side of the road. She was a single mother working two jobs to make ends meet, and her car was her lifeline. Without it, she couldn't get to work or take her kids to school. When the mechanic told her the repair bill would be over a thousand dollars, Lisa felt a wave of panic. She didn't have the money, and the thought of missing work and falling further behind on bills was overwhelming.

A coworker, Sam, heard about Lisa's situation and decided to act. Sam knew that Lisa was unlikely to ask for help, so he discreetly started a small fund among their coworkers. Within days, they had collected enough to cover the repair costs. When Sam handed Lisa the envelope with the money, she burst into tears, overcome with gratitude.

With her car repaired, Lisa was able to keep her job and maintain stability for her family. She later shared that the experience inspired her to help others in similar situations whenever she could. What had been a moment of crisis became a turning point, reminding Lisa that she wasn't alone and that even a small act of kindness could create profound change.

## THE POWER OF EMERGENCY AID

Emergency aid provides immediate relief during life's most challenging moments. Whether it's covering medical bills, repairing a vehicle, or paying overdue utility bills, these gestures can prevent a temporary setback from turning into a long-term crisis. Offering financial assistance in times of need is not just about solving a problem—it's about showing compassion and creating a safety net for others.

## PRACTICAL WAYS TO PROVIDE EMERGENCY AID

- **Crowdfunding Platforms:** Contribute to campaigns for individuals facing medical emergencies, housing crises, or other unexpected expenses.

- **Community Emergency Funds:** Start or contribute to a local fund dedicated to helping neighbors in need.
- **Offer Direct Help:** If you personally know someone facing a financial challenge, offer to cover part of their expenses directly.
- **Utility Assistance Programs:** Partner with organizations that help families keep the lights on and the water running during tough times.
- **Car Repairs:** Work with local mechanics to set up a fund for discounted or free repairs for those in need.
- **Gift Cards for Essentials:** Provide gift cards for gas, groceries, or pharmacies to offer immediate support.
- **Pay It Forward:** Anonymously pay someone's bill or repair cost through an intermediary, such as a landlord or service provider.
- **Partner with Local Businesses:** Collaborate with local businesses to sponsor emergency assistance programs for the community.

## THE RIPPLE EFFECT OF EMERGENCY AID

When Sam and his coworkers helped Lisa, they didn't just fix her car—they restored her hope in humanity and gave her stability. Lisa's gratitude turned into a commitment to help others, creating a ripple effect of kindness. Emergency aid not only alleviates immediate stress but also reinforces the idea that people are not alone in their struggles.

By offering help during a crisis, you're doing more than solving a problem. You're creating a bridge to resilience and inspiring others to pay it forward. Whether it's a small donation or a coordinated community effort to help with medical bills, car repairs, or utility payments, emergency aid reminds us of the profound impact we can have when we step up for one another.

CHAPTER 8

# *Scholarships*

THE RESIDENT OF a small, rural town, Ava was a high school senior with big dreams of becoming a nurse. She excelled academically and often stayed after school to help tutor her classmates. However, Ava's family struggled financially, and the prospect of paying for college seemed out of reach. Her parents worked tirelessly to support the family, but saving for tuition seemed like an impossible challenge.

One evening, Ava's science teacher, Mr. Johnson, shared her story with the local community at a town hall meeting. Inspired by Ava's dedication and potential, the community came together to create a scholarship fund in her name. Local businesses donated a portion of their earnings, individuals contributed what they could, and the town organized fundraisers like bake sales and a charity walk.

When Ava was awarded the scholarship, she couldn't believe it. The community's generosity had given her the opportunity to attend nursing school. Four years later, Ava returned to her hometown as a registered nurse, working at the local clinic and caring for the very people who had supported her and helped her achieve her dream.

## THE POWER OF SCHOLARSHIPS

Scholarships represent more than financial aid—they are investments into someone's future. They provide opportunities for education, personal growth, and career development, breaking down barriers that might otherwise hold someone back. For recipients like Ava, scholarships can open doors to achieving dreams and making a lasting impact in their communities.

## PRACTICAL WAYS TO CONTRIBUTE TO SCHOLARSHIPS

- **Pool Resources:** Single individuals and families who have chosen not to have children can pool their resources to provide scholarship funds for the child of a friend's family.

- **Create a Community Fund:** Collaborate with local businesses and neighbors to establish a scholarship fund for students in need.
- **Partner with Schools:** Work with high schools, colleges, or vocational programs to identify deserving candidates and provide financial assistance.
- **Organize Fundraisers:** Host events like silent auctions, car washes, or charity runs to raise money for scholarships.
- **Crowdfunding Campaigns:** Use platforms like GoFundMe or Kickstarter to pool resources and reach a broader audience.
- **Employer Contributions:** Encourage local businesses to sponsor scholarships for family members of employees.
- **Alumni Networks:** Engage alumni from schools or universities to contribute to scholarship funds for future students.
- **Target Specific Needs:** Create scholarships tailored to specific groups, such as single parents, veterans, or first-generation college students.

- **Offer Micro Scholarships:** Contribute smaller amounts to cover textbooks, supplies, or certification fees for students.

## THE RIPPLE EFFECT OF SCHOLARSHIPS

By investing in Ava's education, the community not only helped her achieve her dream but also gained a dedicated healthcare provider who gave back tenfold. Scholarships have the potential to transform lives, elevate families, and strengthen communities. By pooling resources to sponsor education, we empower individuals to break cycles of poverty and achieve their full potential. Whether it's a small contribution or a larger effort, your support can help someone turn their aspirations into reality, leaving a legacy of hope and opportunity.

CHAPTER 9

# *Food Pantries*

On a cold November evening, Brianna, a single mother of three, found herself staring at empty kitchen cabinets. With her hours cut at work and bills piling up, she was struggling to put food on the table. Feeling desperate, she remembered a flyer she had seen about a local food pantry and decided to visit it the next day.

When Brianna arrived at the pantry, she was greeted warmly by volunteers who handed her bags filled with fresh produce, canned goods, and other staples. For the first time in weeks, she felt a sense of relief. She was able to prepare a hearty meal for her family that evening, and the joy on her children's faces as they sat down to eat filled her with gratitude.

What Brianna didn't know was that the pantry was

supported by donations from people in her community. One of them was Raj, a retired teacher who donated part of his pension each month to help fund the pantry. Raj believed no one in his town should go hungry, and he also volunteered at the pantry to stock shelves and distribute food.

Later that year, Brianna, now back on her feet after securing a new job, returned to the pantry—not as a client but as a volunteer. She wanted to give back to the place that had supported her during her hardest times, and she joined Raj and other volunteers to ensure no one in their community would go hungry.

## THE POWER OF FOOD PANTRIES

Food pantries are often a quiet lifeline for people who are doing their best but still falling short. Providing more than just food, they also offer relief, dignity, and the reassurance that someone cares. For many families, having access to a food pantry means they do not have to choose between buying groceries and paying the electric bill.

When we support food pantries, we help stabilize lives. A stocked shelf or a simple donation can ease stress, create breathing room, and give families the chance to focus on getting through a hard season. These small acts of support remind people that they are not alone and that help can show up in simple, practical ways—one bag of groceries at a time.

## PRACTICAL WAYS TO SUPPORT FOOD PANTRIES

- **Donate Nonperishable Goods to Local Food Banks or Pantries:** Canned vegetables, pasta, rice, and other long-lasting items are always in demand.
- **Provide Fresh Produce:** Many pantries accept fresh fruits and vegetables, offering clients healthier options.
- **Contribute Financially:** Monetary donations allow pantries to purchase specific items in bulk or fill gaps in inventory.
- **Organize a Food Drive:** Rally your workplace, school, or neighborhood to collect donations for a local food pantry.
- **Volunteer Your Time:** Help sort, pack, or distribute items at a food pantry or during community events.

- **Offer Specialty Items:** Donate baby formula, diapers, or pet food to address the diverse needs within the community.
- **Corporate Partnerships:** Encourage local businesses to donate surplus food or sponsor food pantry initiatives.
- **Spread Awareness:** Share information about food pantries on social media or distribute flyers in your community.

## THE RIPPLE EFFECT OF FOOD PANTRIES

Brianna's story highlights how food pantry support can change lives. What started as a simple act of generosity from Raj and others created a chain of giving that gave Brianna and her children nourishment and hope and inspired her to help others. Food pantries do more than alleviate hunger—they build connections and foster resilience within communities.

When you contribute to a food pantry, you're not just providing meals; you're investing in your neighbors' well-being and empowering them to overcome challenges. Every bag of groceries given, every dollar donated, and every hour volunteered creates ripples of kindness that nourish both bodies and spirits.

## CHAPTER 10

# *Transportation Assistance*

JAKE WAS A hardworking barista who dreamed of becoming a teacher. He had recently been accepted into a certification program, but there was a problem—his car had broken down, and he couldn't afford the repairs. Without reliable transportation, he missed several classes and was on the verge of dropping out.

One day, while Jake was venting to a regular customer, Ivy, she asked if he had ever used rideshare services. Jake admitted he couldn't afford them regularly. Ivy, a former educator herself, empathized with his situation and decided to help. That afternoon, she purchased a prepaid rideshare gift card and handed it to Jake. "This should help you get to your classes," she said with a kind smile.

Jake was hesitant at first but gratefully accepted. The card covered his rides for several weeks, allowing him to attend all his classes and even pick up extra shifts at work. Ivy's gesture not only eased his immediate stress but also renewed his determination to succeed. Years later, Jake earned his teaching certification and secured a position at a local school. Remembering Ivy's generosity, he created a small fund with his first paycheck to help students and colleagues who were facing their own transportation challenges.

## THE POWER OF TRANSPORTATION ASSISTANCE

Access to reliable transportation is essential for education, work, and healthcare. For many, the lack of affordable or dependable transit options can be a barrier to achieving their goals. Offering transportation assistance, even in small ways, can help bridge this gap and provide individuals with opportunities to improve their circumstances.

## PRACTICAL WAYS TO PROVIDE TRANSPORTATION ASSISTANCE

- **Prepaid Rideshare Gift Cards:** Purchase rideshare gift cards and give them to someone in need of a way to commute to work, school, or appointments.

- **Public Transit Passes:** Donate bus or train passes to local shelters, schools, or community centers.
- **Carpooling:** Offer to drive someone to work, school, or appointments if it fits your schedule.
- **Gas Cards:** Provide prepaid fuel cards to individuals or families struggling with transportation costs.
- **Cover Transportation Cost:** Offer to cover a rideshare or public transportation fare for someone without reliable access.
- **Workplace Support:** Encourage your employer to subsidize transportation for employees or provide shuttle services.
- **Community Ride Programs:** Organize a volunteer-based program where neighbors can share rides with those in need.
- **Collaborate with Nonprofits:** Partner with local organizations to fund transportation services for vulnerable populations.

- **Help with Repairs:** Assist someone with car repairs, either through direct financial help or by connecting them with affordable mechanics.

## THE RIPPLE EFFECT OF TRANSPORTATION ASSISTANCE

Ivy's act of kindness didn't just help Jake get to his classes, it allowed him to achieve his goals and later pay it forward to others. Transportation assistance can remove obstacles that might otherwise seem insurmountable, empowering individuals to pursue education, maintain employment, and access critical services.

When you offer transportation assistance, you're providing more than just a ride; you're giving someone the freedom to move forward in life. Whether it's covering a single fare or creating a long-term solution, these small acts of generosity can open doors to opportunities that change lives.

## CHAPTER 11

# *Holiday Support*

THE HOLIDAYS HAD always been a difficult time for Rebecca and her two children, Peyton and Noah. After losing her job earlier in the year, Rebecca was struggling to make ends meet, and the thought of providing gifts or a special meal for her kids seemed impossible. She worried that the holidays would only serve as a painful reminder of what they lacked.

Meanwhile, across town, Rachel was organizing her annual "Adopt a Family" holiday program through her local community center. Families in need would submit wish lists, and volunteers would step in to provide gifts, food, and other holiday essentials. One of the lists belonged to Rebecca's family.

Rachel and her friends went above and beyond.

They purchased toys for Peyton and Noah, a warm coat and boots for Rebecca, and stocked a box with all the ingredients needed for a festive meal. They even included a small Christmas tree with ornaments to brighten their home. On Christmas Eve, volunteers delivered the items to Rebecca's doorstep, leaving her in tears of gratitude.

That evening, as Peyton and Noah excitedly opened their gifts and the family shared a warm meal together, Rebecca felt something she hadn't in a long time: hope. The generosity of strangers reminded her that she wasn't alone, and it inspired her to give back when she was able. The next year, after finding stable work, Rebecca joined Rachel's program as a volunteer, paying forward the kindness she had received and helping make happy holiday memories for another struggling family.

## THE POWER OF HOLIDAY SUPPORT

The holidays can be a time of joy, but for many families, they're a source of stress and sadness due to financial hardships. Providing holiday support ensures that families in need can experience the warmth, celebration, and connection that make this season special.

These gestures can alleviate stress and create cherished memories, leaving a lasting impact. Even small acts, like giving a gift card, a meal, or a thoughtfully chosen present, can restore a sense of normalcy and hope during a difficult time. When families feel supported, the holidays become a reminder of compassion rather than a season of worry.

## PRACTICAL WAYS TO PROVIDE HOLIDAY SUPPORT

- **Adopt-a-Family Programs:** Participate in local or online programs through which you can sponsor a family by fulfilling their holiday wish list.
- **Food Baskets:** Prepare and deliver holiday meal kits, including ingredients for a traditional feast, to families in need.
- **Toy Drives:** Donate new toys to organizations like Toys for Tots or local community centers to brighten a child's holiday.
- **Secret Santa:** Organize or take part in a Secret Santa event for a shelter or community group, ensuring everyone receives a gift this season.

- **Holiday Gift Cards:** Provide gift cards for groceries, clothing stores, or big-box retailers so families can purchase what they need most.
- **Winter Essentials:** Donate warm clothing, blankets, and boots to keep families cozy during the coldest months.
- **Host a Holiday Party:** Organize a festive event at a community center or shelter, complete with decorations, music, and treats.
- **Include Personalized Notes:** Add handwritten holiday cards to your gifts to share encouragement and festive cheer.
- **Sponsor a Child's Wish List:** Work with schools or nonprofits to fulfill specific holiday wishes for children in need.
- **Collaborate with Local Businesses:** Partner with businesses to sponsor larger-scale holiday support efforts, such as free meals or gift giveaways.

## THE RIPPLE EFFECT OF HOLIDAY SUPPORT

Rachel's efforts didn't just brighten Rebecca's holiday—they gave her the strength to persevere and eventually join the effort to help others. Holiday support has the power to restore dignity and bring joy during a time that can feel isolating for those in need. The small act of providing gifts or a meal can create lifelong memories and inspire recipients to give back in the future.

When you sponsor a family during the holidays, you're doing more than just providing material support. You're offering hope, showing compassion, and reminding others that they're part of a caring community. These small acts of kindness help make the holidays a time of joy and connection for everyone.

## CHAPTER 12

# *Animal Shelters*

KEISHA HAD ALWAYS been an animal lover, and her dog, Max, was her constant companion. One rainy afternoon, while scrolling social media, she saw a post from her local animal shelter. They were running low on supplies and needed donations of pet food, blankets, and funds to cover veterinary expenses for a recent influx of rescued animals. The images of the animals—wide-eyed kittens, scruffy dogs, a recovering injured rabbit—tugged at her heart.

Keisha decided to act. She reached out to her friends and family, sharing the shelter's needs and organizing a donation drive. Within days, her garage was filled with bags of pet food, toys, blankets, and even cleaning supplies. Keisha also contributed funds to cover the veterinary care of a senior dog named Bella, who had been neglected and was requiring extensive medical treatment.

When Keisha visited the shelter to drop off the donations, she met Bella, who wagged her tail timidly and leaned into Keisha's hand for a pet. The shelter staff shared how the donations had eased their burden, allowing them to focus on finding homes for the animals. A few weeks later, Keisha learned that Bella had been adopted by a loving family and was now healthy and happy thanks to the care she was receiving.

## THE POWER OF ANIMAL SHELTERS

Animal shelters provide essential care for abandoned, neglected, and stray animals, but they often operate with limited resources. Donations of supplies, food, and funds help shelters meet the needs of these animals, from daily care to critical medical treatment. Supporting shelters not only improves the lives of animals but also increases their chances of being adopted into forever homes.

## PRACTICAL WAYS TO SUPPORT ANIMAL SHELTERS

- **Donate Supplies:** Contribute pet food, toys, blankets, cleaning products, and crates to local shelters.
- **Cover Veterinary Expenses:** Provide funds to help with spay/neuter surgeries, vaccinations, or emergency medical care for injured animals.
- **Sponsor an Animal:** Pay for the care of a specific animal until it's adopted.
- **Organize Drives:** Host a donation drive in your community to collect supplies for shelters.
- **Volunteer Your Time:** Help with tasks like walking dogs, cleaning kennels, or assisting at adoption events.
- **Foster Pets:** Offer temporary homes for animals that need extra care or socialization before adoption.
- **Spread Awareness:** Share shelter updates and adoptable animals on social media accounts to increase visibility.

- **Partner with Local Businesses:** Encourage businesses to sponsor shelters or match donations during fundraising events.
- **Adopt Responsibly:** If you're ready for a pet, consider adopting from a shelter to give an animal a second chance.
- **Support Spay/Neuter Programs:** Fund or advocate for initiatives that reduce overpopulation.

## THE RIPPLE EFFECT OF ANIMAL SHELTERS

Keisha's story illustrates how one act of kindness can create ripples of impact. Her efforts not only improved the shelter's conditions but also played a role in Bella's recovery and adoption. Animal shelters thrive on community support, and even small contributions can make a significant difference.

When you donate to or volunteer at an animal shelter, you're providing more than just material aid—you're giving animals a chance to feel safe, loved, and valued. Whether it's a bag of food, a monetary contribution, or a few hours of your time, your support helps create a better future for animals in need and inspires others to care for the animals in their community.

## CHAPTER 13

# *Cultural Access*

SOPHIA WORKED AS a high school art teacher in a low-income community, where many of her students had never set foot in a museum or theater. One day, while discussing famous artists, she noticed a spark in her student Mateo. He was captivated by the idea of seeing a real Van Gogh painting but quickly dismissed it with a shrug. "I'll never be able to go to a place like that," he said quietly.

Determined to change that, Sophia reached out to her friends and some local businesses, explaining her mission to provide cultural experiences for her students. A local foundation stepped in to donate tickets to the city's art museum, and Sophia used her own funds to cover transportation costs.

The day of the trip was unforgettable. For many

of the students, it was their first time visiting a museum. Mateo stood in front of Van Gogh's *Starry Night* with wide eyes, whispering, "I never thought I'd see something like this in real life." The experience ignited a passion in him, and he began to take his art assignments more seriously, even staying after school to work on his paintings.

Years later, Mateo became an art teacher himself, inspiring a new generation of students. He often credited that museum visit as the moment that changed his perspective, showing him that art wasn't just something in books, but was a world he could be a part of.

## THE POWER OF CULTURAL ACCESS

Access to cultural experiences like museums, theaters, and historical sites has the power to inspire creativity, broaden horizons, and instill a sense of belonging. For individuals who wouldn't otherwise have the means, these opportunities can be transformative, sparking passions and opening doors to new possibilities. A single visit can change how someone sees the world or themselves within it. When people feel welcomed into spaces of learning and expression, they gain confidence, curiosity, and a deeper connection to the community around them.

## PRACTICAL WAYS TO PROVIDE CULTURAL ACCESS

- **Purchase Tickets:** Provide museum tickets, theater passes, or other cultural experiences for someone who couldn't otherwise afford them.
- **Donate Tickets:** Purchase and donate museum or theater tickets to schools, community groups, or local nonprofits.
- **Sponsor a Field Trip:** Partner with educators to fund transportation and admission for students to visit cultural institutions.
- **Gift Passes:** Provide annual memberships or passes to cultural institutions for families in need.
- **Organize Group Outings:** Coordinate group visits for underserved communities, covering the cost of tickets and transportation.
- **Partner with Organizations:** Work with cultural institutions to sponsor free admission days or discounted rates for specific groups.
- **Support Community Events:** Publicize or organize events like art fairs, outdoor concerts, or public theater performances.

- **Fund Workshops:** Sponsor hands-on workshops at cultural centers, giving participants a chance to engage creatively.
- **Promote Accessibility:** Advocate for inclusive programs that ensure cultural institutions are welcoming to all, including those with disabilities or language barriers.

## THE RIPPLE EFFECT OF CULTURAL ACCESS

Sophia's effort to bring her students to the art museum didn't just impact Mateo—it planted seeds of inspiration in an entire group of young minds. Access to cultural experiences fosters not only individual growth but also instills a deeper appreciation for history, art, and community. These experiences can bridge gaps in understanding and spark lifelong interests.

By providing cultural access, you're giving more than just a ticket—you're offering a glimpse into a world of possibility. Whether it's a museum visit, a theater performance, or an art workshop, these moments can leave lasting impressions, transforming perspectives and opening doors to dreams that once seemed unattainable.

CHAPTER 14

# *Subscription Services*

WHEN LAUREN LOST her job during a company downsizing, she found herself struggling to make ends meet. With bills piling up, she couldn't justify spending money on anything beyond the basics. Her lifelong dream of improving her graphic design skills felt increasingly out of reach, as even enrolling in an online course was beyond her budget.

One day, Lauren's friend Jess heard about her struggles and decided to help. Knowing Lauren's passion for design, Jess gifted her a one-year subscription to an online learning platform that offered courses in graphic design, illustration, and other creative fields. Lauren was overwhelmed by Jess's thoughtful gesture but wasn't sure if she could succeed. Jess reassured her, "Take it one step at a time. You've got this."

Lauren started small, taking beginner courses in digital illustration. With each lesson, her confidence grew. Within months, she had built an impressive portfolio and began freelancing part-time, eventually securing enough projects to replace her lost income. The subscription not only gave her new skills but also restored her sense of purpose and self-worth.

Lauren eventually became a successful freelance designer who did work for many clients, and she often reflected on Jess's gift as the turning point in her career. Inspired by her own journey, she began gifting subscriptions to others who wanted to learn or explore new passions but lacked the resources.

## THE POWER OF SUBSCRIPTION SERVICES

A subscription service may seem like a small gift, but it can have a profound impact. Educational platforms can empower someone to learn new skills, fitness apps can encourage healthier habits, and streaming services can provide much-needed relaxation during stressful times. These subscriptions are not just conveniences—they're opportunities for growth, self-care, and transformation.

## PRACTICAL WAYS TO GIFT SUBSCRIPTION SERVICES

- **Educational Platforms:** Provide access to sites like LinkedIn Learning, MasterClass, Coursera, or Skillshare for skill-building and professional development.
- **Fitness Apps:** Offer subscriptions to fitness platforms like Peloton, Runna, or Yoga with Adriene to promote physical and mental well-being.
- **Streaming Services:** Gift streaming services like Netflix, Disney+, or Spotify to provide entertainment and relaxation.
- **Language Learning Apps:** Share subscriptions to Duolingo, Babbel, or Rosetta Stone to help someone learn a new language.
- **Kids' Platforms:** Support families by gifting subscriptions to educational apps like ABC-mouse or Tynker to help support children's learning and creativity.

- **Hobby-Based Services:** Offer access to niche platforms for interests, such as photography courses on Skillshare, cooking classes through MasterClass, music production tools like Soundtrap or GarageBand, or art tutorials available on platforms like Domestika or YouTube Premium.
- **Book and Audiobook Services:** Gift memberships to Audible, Scribd, or Kindle Unlimited to encourage reading and learning.
- **Subscription Boxes:** Provide curated subscription boxes for wellness, crafts, or self-care, such as calmbox, TheraBox, FabFitFun, KiwiCo craft kits, or Book of the Month, offering something positive to look forward to each month.
- **Mental Health Apps:** Offer services like BetterHelp, Headspace, or Calm to support emotional well-being.

## THE RIPPLE EFFECT OF SUBSCRIPTION SERVICES

Jess's gift of a subscription service didn't just help Lauren learn graphic design—it gave her the tools and confidence to rebuild her life. Subscriptions open doors to new possibilities, helping recipients develop skills, reduce stress, and explore passions they might never have pursued otherwise.

When you gift a subscription service, you're investing in someone's growth and happiness. It's a gesture that can have a lasting impact, encouraging personal transformation and inspiring others to pay it forward. Whether it's for education, fitness, or relaxation, this small but thoughtful gift can make a big difference in another person's journey.

CHAPTER 15

# *Microloans*

In a rural village in Kenya, Amina dreamed of expanding her small roadside produce stand into a thriving market stall. She had the ambition and work ethic, but what she lacked was access to the capital needed to purchase a larger variety of fruits and vegetables. Traditional banks wouldn't offer her a loan because her income was too modest, and local lenders were charging exorbitant interest rates.

One day, Amina learned about a microfinance initiative that provided small loans to entrepreneurs in underserved areas. She applied for a loan of three hundred dollars to buy additional produce and a sturdy tent to protect her goods from the sun and rain. Her application was approved, and within weeks, she transformed her roadside stand into a vibrant, well-stocked market stall.

With her expanded inventory, Amina began attracting more customers, increasing her income significantly. She paid back the loan within six months, and with her savings she hired two assistants, further boosting her business. The additional income allowed her to send her children to school and invest in their future.

What Amina didn't know was that her microloan had been funded by a group of individuals thousands of miles away. People like Tom, a retired accountant who lived in the United States, had contributed small amounts through a microfinance platform, enabling entrepreneurs like Amina to pursue their dreams. Inspired by the impact of his contributions, Tom continued to participate in microloan initiatives, knowing his support was changing lives.

## THE POWER OF MICROLOANS

Microloans provide a lifeline for entrepreneurs in underserved areas, empowering them to build businesses, support their families, and uplift their communities. These small loans, often ranging from $25 to $500, can create ripple effects of economic and social development, helping break the cycle of poverty in the world's most struggling areas.

## PRACTICAL WAYS TO PARTICIPATE IN MICROLOAN PROGRAMS

- **Use Microfinance Platforms:** Join platforms like Kiva or Zidisha to help fund loans for entrepreneurs around the world.
- **Focus on Sustainable Ventures:** Support businesses that promote sustainable practices or address social and environmental issues.
- **Empower Women:** Many microloan recipients are women, who often reinvest their earnings into their families and communities.
- **Collaborate Locally:** Partner with community organizations that provide microloans in your area to help underserved entrepreneurs.
- **Offer Expertise:** Provide mentorship or business advice to loan recipients to maximize their chances of success.
- **Recurring Contributions:** Set up regular contributions to fund new loans as previous ones are repaid.
- **Encourage Group Funding:** Organize friends, coworkers, or community groups to collectively support larger microloan projects.

## THE RIPPLE EFFECT OF MICROLOANS

Amina's story highlights the transformative power of microloans. Her success not only improved her family's quality of life but also contributed to the local economy by creating jobs and attracting more customers to the market. Microloans empower individuals to take control of their futures, fostering resilience and independence.

By participating in microfinance initiatives, you're doing more than lending money—you're investing in human potential. Each loan represents an opportunity for someone to achieve their dreams, provide for their loved ones, and inspire others to follow suit. These small contributions create ripples of hope and opportunity, proving that even the smallest investment can yield a profound impact.

## CHAPTER 16

# *Points and Rewards*

When Melissa opened her credit card app one evening, she noticed she had over 75,000 unused reward points. Normally, she would have redeemed them for a new gadget or airline miles, but this time she hesitated. She had just read a social media post from a young couple in her church who were struggling to afford diapers for their newborn.

Curious, Melissa checked the credit card company's redemption options and discovered she could use her points to purchase a year's supply of diapers. Without spending a single dollar, she placed the order and had the boxes shipped directly to the family's doorstep. A few days later, she received a message filled with gratitude, tears, and emojis. For that couple, Melissa's "nothing" was a lifeline that eased their financial worries and gave them the breathing room to focus on their new baby.

Inspired by that experience, Melissa began using her points intentionally. She redeemed gift cards for groceries and school supplies, donated airline miles to medical transport programs, and encouraged friends to do the same. What once felt like a small, insignificant perk became her favorite way to give back, a quiet but powerful form of generosity that required no extra money, only mindfulness.

## THE POWER OF POINTS AND REWARDS

Points and rewards systems offered by credit cards, loyalty programs, and shopping apps often go unused or unnoticed. Yet they carry real financial value and the power to meet tangible needs.

Redeeming these rewards for essential goods, gift cards, or charitable donations transforms idle value into meaningful impact. A few thousand points can feed a family, supply a classroom, support a shelter, or even fund emergency travel for those in crisis.

Most importantly, sharing points sends a deeper message: Compassion lives in the small spaces of everyday life. When people realize that generosity doesn't have to come from abundance, they begin to see how much they already have to give.

## PRACTICAL WAYS TO HELP OTHERS WITH POINTS AND REWARDS

- **Redeem for Essentials:** Use points and rewards to purchase groceries, diapers, toiletries, or school supplies for families in need.
- **Use Gift Cards for Flexibility:** Many programs allow you to redeem points for gift cards, which can be used to purchase necessities like gas, food, and clothing.
- **Support Shelters:** Donate pet supplies, blankets, or food purchased with points to local animal or homeless shelters.
- **Donate Directly:** Some programs partner with charities, allowing you to donate points or miles directly to organizations like the Red Cross or the Make-A-Wish Foundation.
- **Organize Group Giving:** Encourage your friends, coworkers, or neighbors to pool their unused points for a collective cause.

- **Give Seasonally:** Around the holidays or back-to-school time, redeem points for care packages or supplies that make a timely difference.
- **Share Your Story:** Posting about your experience online or talking about it to those in your community can inspire others to turn their "extras" into acts of kindness.

## THE RIPPLE EFFECT OF POINTS AND REWARDS

Melissa's simple gift of diapers for a needy family sparked a trend in her church. Soon others began donating their own points to help new parents and struggling families. It doesn't take much for generosity to multiply. When one person discovers how easy it is to help, others follow. What began as a few clicks can evolve into community-wide impact, with families fed, animals comforted, students equipped, and spirits lifted.

Points and rewards may seem trivial, but when they are used with purpose, they become a powerful expression of love in action. In a world often defined by scarcity, these small gestures remind us that abundance is not measured by what we own but by what we're willing to share.

## CHAPTER 17

# *Supporting Small Organizations*

SUPPORTING ORGANIZATIONS and small businesses is about more than providing resources—it's a way to cultivate resilience, offer immediate relief, and forge meaningful connections. Each effort, no matter how small it may seem, has the potential to transform lives. Whether it's donating to a local charity, championing a small business, or lending a hand during a crisis, these acts of compassion create ripples that extend far beyond the initial gesture.

Sometimes something as simple as a tent or sleeping bag can make all the difference to someone who has been displaced by a disaster. Supporting small businesses directly sustains livelihoods and strengthens families, serving as a lifeline for communities. These seemingly modest actions often catalyze lasting change.

In 2019, Charlotte found herself in the unique position to make a difference through her company. Every year, she was in charge of dedicating a portion of her company's resources to a cause that resonated with their values and aligned with the spirit of their events. For the 2020 event in Nashville, Tennessee, she grappled with the task of choosing which organization to support. Many people would assume this to be a straightforward decision, but the reality was far more complex. Selecting a charity was not just about giving; it was about ensuring that the contributions created meaningful and sustainable impacts.

For months, Charlotte deliberated, consulted colleagues, and carefully weighed suggestions. One name consistently surfaced during conversations: Candy Christmas (yes, that was her name). Friends and associates encouraged Charlotte to meet with Candy, and their insistence was well-founded.

Candy was an extraordinary individual. Petite in stature, with striking black hair and eyes that radiated love and gratitude, she possessed a warmth that was immediately disarming. Her smile was like a beacon, illuminating every room she entered. But beyond her presence lay an unparalleled passion for serving the homeless and underprivileged. Her dedication was both inspiring and contagious, and Charlotte knew from their first meeting that Candy was someone she needed to work with. They met at the Gaylord Opryland Resort, a serene setting with lush gardens and the sound of cascading water, the perfect backdrop for their conversation. As they talked, Charlotte shared a personal mantra that guided her approach to giving: *Giving back is everyone's responsibility.* Candy resonated deeply with this sentiment, and together with her associate, Burton, they began brainstorming ways to support Candy's organization, The Bridge Ministry.

The Bridge Ministry provided food, clothing, and essential supplies to Nashville's homeless population. More than that, it offered hope and compassion to those who needed it most. After careful discussion, they decided on a tangible and immediate action: purchasing tents and sleeping bags for the homeless. These items were not just practical; they represented safety, warmth, and dignity. Charlotte placed an order for hundreds of tents and sleeping bags, eager to see their plan come to fruition. What they didn't anticipate was how quickly the items would arrive: Three pallets of supplies showed up at Charlotte's office weeks ahead of schedule.

The early arrival posed a logistical challenge. Charlotte realized there wasn't enough space on the truck designated to transport the supplies alongside their event materials. It was then that she learned one of her coworkers was celebrating an anniversary. A solution quickly took shape: She proposed the couple deliver the supplies to Nashville early, using the opportunity to enjoy a few days exploring the city as they celebrated their anniversary.

This arrangement was a win-win. Charlotte's coworker was delighted with the chance to stay at the Gaylord Opryland Resort and experience its breathtaking atriums and warm hospitality. Meanwhile, the tents and sleeping bags reached Nashville ahead of schedule. At the time, it felt like a minor adjustment to their plans—a small logistical fix. Little did they know it would become so much more.

## THE POWER OF SUPPORTING SMALL ORGANIZATIONS

It's important to trust that quiet nudge inside us—the intuition or higher power that guides us to act, even when we don't fully understand why. Delivering the supplies for The Bridge Ministry early was a small decision, but it turned out to be exactly what was needed. Supporting grassroots organizations is about more than making donations. It's about understanding the needs of a community, acting with intention, and being willing to step up when it matters most.

## PRACTICAL WAYS TO SUPPORT SMALL ORGANIZATIONS

- **Start Local:** Identify nonprofits, ministries, and small businesses in your own community that align with your values. Local impact is often immediate, visible, and deeply personal.
- **Ask What's Needed Most:** Before donating, take the time to listen. Sometimes organizations need funding, but often they need supplies, volunteers, or even professional expertise. Meeting the *actual* need makes your contribution more powerful.
- **Offer Skills, Not Just Money:** Small businesses and nonprofits benefit from expertise in areas like marketing, accounting, logistics, or IT. A

few hours of your time can save them hundreds of dollars and strengthen their operations.

- **Support Through Spending:** Choose to buy from small, local businesses whenever possible. Every purchase helps sustain jobs, families, and community resilience—especially during times of crisis.
- **Build Partnerships, Not One-Time Gifts:** Lasting relationships with local organizations or ministries create long-term impact. Check in regularly, share resources, and collaborate on projects that make a difference year-round.
- **Empower Employees to Give Back:** Encourage your company or workplace to dedicate a portion of its time or budget to community causes. Group volunteering or donation drives build team unity and magnify your collective reach.
- **Trust Your Intuition:** Pay attention to those quiet nudges that guide you toward action. Often, the most meaningful giving opportunities come through unexpected situations or small logistical "detours."

- **Respond Quickly in Crisis:** In moments of disaster or hardship, fast action saves lives. Keep a list of trusted local organizations—like The Bridge Ministry—so you're ready to mobilize help when it's needed most.
- **Celebrate the Wins:** Share stories of the impact your contributions create. When others see tangible results—like tents that become shelter during a storm—they're inspired to join in and multiply the good.
- **Remember: No Act Is Too Small:** Whether it's purchasing a tent, buying a meal from a struggling café, or donating leftover event supplies, your "nothing" can become someone else's everything when offered with intention and compassion.

## THE RIPPLE EFFECT OF SUPPORTING SMALL ORGANIZATIONS

Just one week after the delivery of supplies to The Bridge Ministry, a series of devastating tornadoes tore through Tennessee. The destruction was catastrophic: Homes were flattened, entire neighborhoods were leveled, and twenty-four lives were lost. The area surrounding Nashville, where the ministry operates, was hit particularly hard.

Amid the chaos, Candy and her team sprang into action. They braved heavy rain and exhaustion to distribute tents and sleeping bags. These supplies became lifelines for hundreds of people who had lost everything. It was humbling to see how something so simple could provide comfort, security, and hope in the face of such devastation. The tornadoes were followed by the COVID-19 pandemic, which brought cleanup and recovery efforts to a standstill. For many displaced families, the supplies provided by The Bridge Ministry were their only source of refuge during those dark months. In a moment no one could have predicted, an early delivery turned into a lifeline, reminding everyone that small acts, given at the right time, can change everything.

SECTION TWO

# TIME NOTHINGS

# *When Time Becomes a Gift*

Time is an essential resource, but many of us fail to recognize it as a valuable asset that creates meaningful change. However, time is actually our *most* valuable resource because it cannot be replaced or restored, which makes it a priceless gift. How we use our time can have a major effect on others, even though our individual actions may seem small or insignificant. The acts of kindness that we often think of as nothing have the ability to produce enduring waves of connection, support, and encouragement.

Consider the power of simply being present. The practice of giving someone your complete attention is an incredibly valuable gesture in today's world because people experience distractions everywhere they go. The small investments of time we dedicate to others through active listening, meal sharing, or note writing create immeasurable impact.

When we choose to give our time, it shows that we value people. The practice of showing kindness through small actions strengthens social bonds while developing a supportive community that's based on compassion. Time-based giving allows everyone to participate in making this world a better place for others, because all of us have some amount time that we can dedicate to creating positive and lasting change.

## CHAPTER 18

# *Active Listening*

One December evening, Carmen sat working in her favorite coffee shop, surrounded by the low hum of conversation and the familiar comfort of warm drinks and soft lighting. When the barista, Lily, delivered her a second cup of coffee, Carmen noticed that something seemed off with Lily. Her shoulders were tense, her movements slower than usual. The cheerful energy she normally carried was missing, replaced by visible fatigue. Her eyes held a quiet heaviness that caught Carmen's attention.

As Lily reached to clear an empty cup from a nearby table, Carmen gently asked, "How's your day going?" The question seemed to catch Lily off guard. She offered a polite smile and replied, "I'm okay," though the words didn't quite match her expression.

Carmen closed her laptop and looked up at Lily. "Are you really doing okay? You look like you could use a friend." That simple question opened something Lily had been holding in. Her voice softened as she admitted that the past few weeks had been especially difficult.

Inviting Lily to sit down for a moment, Carmen assured her she had time to listen to anything she felt comfortable sharing. Lily hesitated, then checked in with her coworker at the counter, who waved her off with reassurance. Taking a deep breath, Lily returned to the table, sat down, and began to share her story. Her mother had recently received a serious medical diagnosis, and Lily had stepped into the role of caregiver while continuing to work long hours at the café. Between hospital visits, appointments, college coursework, and the loneliness that came from having little time for friends, the weight had become overwhelming.

Carmen listened without interrupting or offering solutions. She maintained eye contact, nodded in understanding, and occasionally responded with quiet affirmations: "That must be incredibly hard." "I'm so sorry you're carrying all of this." "That sounds like a lot." As Lily spoke, the tension in her body slowly eased. By the end of the conversation, her shoulders had relaxed and her voice carried a sense of relief. "I didn't realize how much I needed to say this out loud," she admitted. Her challenges hadn't disappeared, but sharing them with Carmen had lightened the burden.

In the weeks that followed, Lily seemed calmer during Carmen's visits to the café. One afternoon, she handed over a cup of coffee with a small, folded note tucked beneath the saucer. It read, "Thank you for listening. It reminded me that I'm not alone." The moment served as a quiet reminder of the power of active listening. No advice had been given. No problems had been solved. Simply being present had made all the difference.

## THE POWER OF ACTIVE LISTENING

People rarely experience what it's like to truly be heard because most conversations happen quickly while each individual remains preoccupied with other things. The art of active listening, however, demands three essential qualities: patience, empathy, and an open heart. Deep listening is a powerful tool that enables us to create meaningful, positive changes in the lives of others.

The experience of being heard by another person

creates a sense of comfort for us, providing validation that helps us feel less alone while establishing a vital human connection during difficult times. And the practice of nonjudgmental listening, which avoids offering quick-fix responses, enables us to find healing. Through active listening, we validate the human experience of others while demonstrating that their emotions and life events hold significance.

## PRACTICAL WAYS TO BE AN ACTIVE LISTENER

- **Give Your Full Attention:** Put away distractions and focus entirely on the person speaking. Make eye contact and use body language to show you're engaged.
- **Validate Their Feelings:** Acknowledge their emotions with statements like "That must be really hard" or "I can see why you feel that way."
- **Avoid Interrupting:** Let them speak at their own pace without jumping in to share your own experiences or offer solutions. Not everyone is looking for an immediate solution; often, they just want to be heard.

- **Ask Open-Ended Questions:** Encourage the other person to elaborate by asking questions like "How did that make you feel?" or "What do you think would help?"
- **Be Nonjudgmental:** Create a safe space by refraining from offering criticism or unsolicited advice.
- **Follow Up:** If appropriate, check in with them later to see how they're doing. This shows that you genuinely care about them and value their well-being.

## THE RIPPLE EFFECT OF ACTIVE LISTENING

Active listening brings the individual who is sharing their story relief from their emotions while confirming their worth and giving them strength. They begin to understand that their voice holds value and that it's okay for them to share their challenges with others. The listener grows in empathy while strengthening character qualities such as patience and kindness. The practice of active listening helps us move away from problem-solving toward having deeper understanding, which enables us to love more intensely. A society built on active listening creates stronger bonds between individuals while bringing communities together. That's because people who feel heard and understood tend to show greater kindness and compassion toward others. It's a positive cycle that brings more compassion to a world that desperately needs it.

CHAPTER 19

# *Volunteering*

Nyla spent several months driving past an unremarkable brick building, which housed the local community shelter for families in need. While she kept intending to visit the shelter and ask about volunteer opportunities, the regular interruptions of daily life kept getting in the way. Finally, she listened to that inner voice reminding her that she needed to make volunteering a priority and stopped by on a Saturday morning.

She entered the shelter building, where the volunteer coordinator, Margaret, welcomed her. Margaret's friendly demeanor and energetic personality made Nyla feel comfortable right away. "Welcome to our facility." Margaret smiled as she shook Nyla's hand. "We receive our highest number of visitors on Saturdays, as families stop by to access food, clothing, and support." Then she handed Nyla an apron, explaining that they needed volunteers to serve lunch in the kitchen area.

The initial part of her experience caused Nyla to feel a bit uncomfortable. She didn't really know how to interact with the continuous flow of people who were dealing with so much in their lives. The faces of the parents displayed exhaustion, yet they didn't hesitate to express deep appreciation for the help they were receiving. The elderly individuals in the shelter, who needed help for basic needs such as walking, shared their gratitude for the canes and walkers provided for mobility.

Nyla started to observe meaningful connections between people as she distributed food to the visitors. A shy smile appeared on the face of a little girl who clung to her mother's hand. An older man stopped to express his appreciation for the shelter's excellent chili. A young mother shared with her that the shelter had become an essential source of support for her family. Nyla quickly realized that giving her time was bringing positive change to people. The act of showing up and being available to others was just as important—and in some ways, perhaps *more* important—than making a large monetary contribution.

Her next task was organizing donations in the shelter's clothing room, which contained an excessive amount of clothing items, blankets, and shoes that thankfully filled all available shelves. As she sorted the donations into categories, a ten-year-old boy arrived with his father to select a winter coat. After she helped him find the perfect red coat, he expressed his delight by wrapping his arms around the coat and exclaiming, "It's just like Christmas!" His happiness was contagious and brought an immense smile to Nyla's face as she reflected upon how small contributions of time support a much larger purpose beyond our individual efforts.

## THE POWER OF VOLUNTEERING

Shelters, food banks, and community centers depend on volunteers who distribute meals, manage donations, and provide social support to people who are experiencing poverty and loneliness. The recipients of these services often find volunteers to be an important source of optimism and social connection, as they form connections while receiving a hot meal, being gifted with warm clothing, or simply having someone to talk to.

Volunteers may initially think they're giving their

time to assist others, yet the experience also creates significant changes within the volunteer. Empathy is developed as they get to know individuals from different backgrounds, hear their stories, and better understand the challenges they face. What began as a single experience can soon grow into an ongoing commitment. Over time, continued involvement allows meaningful relationships to form with staff, fellow volunteers, and those being served. This ultimately reshapes perspectives on community, compassion, and the vital role social services play in people's lives.

## PRACTICAL WAYS TO VOLUNTEER

- **Local Shelters:** Help serve meals, organize donations, or assist with administrative tasks.
- **Food Banks:** Sort and pack food items, distribute groceries to families in need, or assist with fundraising efforts.
- **Community Centers:** Share your skills by teaching a class, mentoring youth, or helping with events.
- **Animal Shelters:** Walk dogs, clean kennels, or help find forever homes for animals.

- **Schools and Libraries:** Volunteer as a tutor, read to children, or assist with after-school programs.
- **Disaster Relief Organizations:** Join efforts to provide aid during natural disasters by assembling kits or offering on-the-ground support.

## THE RIPPLE EFFECT OF VOLUNTEERING

The effects of volunteering reach further than the actual time spent doing service work. Your efforts help plant seeds of compassion, which grow in remarkable ways. Volunteering creates emotional and spiritual changes that transform individual lives and community structures. Dignity is restored, hope is kindled, and trust is developed.

Many of those who receive assistance later support others, keeping the chain of giving going as people rebuild their lives and their self-worth. Volunteering enables different social groups to work together to create an environment where positive actions spread from person to person. The cumulative effect of these ripples creates extensive networks of compassion, which can transform the fundamental structure of society.

CHAPTER 20

# *Helping with Chores*

On a bright spring afternoon, Lindsay was trimming hedges in a quiet residential neighborhood when she noticed Mrs. Keller across the street struggling to move heavy bags of soil toward her garden. Each step seemed difficult. She paused often to readjust her grip, wiping sweat from her forehead as the weight proved more than she could manage alone.

Mrs. Keller was always kind and friendly to Lindsay, though it appeared that she spent most of her days by herself. Since her husband's passing, the responsibilities he once handled around the house had slowly become overwhelming. The garden they had cared for together, once blooming with roses and daisies, had grown overrun with weeds, and the yard reflected the toll of time and loss.

Seeing her neighbor struggle, Lindsay set down her clippers and walked over. With a warm smile, she asked if the older woman might like some help. Relief immediately crossed Mrs. Keller's face. Together, they carried the bags of soil to the garden, the weight becoming manageable once shared. When they were finished, Mrs. Keller thanked Lindsay, explaining that her aging back had made the task far more difficult than she had expected.

What began as a simple offer to help quickly grew into something more. The garden beds were nearly inaccessible, choked with weeds that had been impossible for her to tackle alone. Lindsay offered to help clear them, and after a brief pause, Mrs. Keller agreed. They spent the afternoon side by side, pulling weeds, planting flowers, and slowly restoring the garden. As they worked, Mrs. Keller shared stories of weekends spent gardening with her husband, recalling how much pride he had taken in their yard. Speaking of those memories brought her visible comfort, and her voice carried warmth as she talked.

As the work continued, other small tasks came into view. The porch needed cleaning, and a loose gutter hung precariously from the roof. One by one, Lindsay helped Mrs. Keller take care of each task. With every completed job, the older woman stood a little taller, her expression growing lighter. By the end of the day, the garden had regained a measure of its former beauty. More importantly, the burden Mrs. Keller had been carrying for months had finally lifted. She expressed her gratitude quietly, her voice unsteady as she admitted she had been avoiding the work because it all felt too overwhelming.

Though Lindsay had come simply to help, the experience proved meaningful for both of them. What started as one neighbor asking the other if she could offer assistance became a reminder of the strength found in shared effort and the sense of community that grows when people are willing to step in, work together, and lighten one another's load.

## THE POWER OF HELPING WITH CHORES

People who are dealing with aging, physical or emotional challenges, illness, or grief often find certain parts of their lives becoming difficult or even unmanageable, including cleaning, organizing, and yard care. Volunteering time to help with chores not only provides physical assistance but also emotional support. It also builds connection and fosters friendship as the previously overwhelming task list is tackled. And those who receive assistance with their own chores are inspired to help others in some way as well.

## PRACTICAL WAYS TO HELP WITH CHORES

- **Start Small:** Offer to assist with a specific task, like mowing the lawn or washing dishes. Sometimes, people hesitate to accept help for fear of imposing, so starting small can ease their concerns.
- **Collaborate:** Turn the chore into a shared activity. This not only makes the task more enjoyable but also creates an opportunity to bond.
- **Be Observant:** Pay attention to signs that someone might need help, like an overgrown yard, a cluttered porch, or a sidewalk full of snow.
- **Enlist Others:** Rally neighbors or friends to tackle bigger projects, like painting a house or deep cleaning a garage.
- **Be Consistent:** Regular check-ins can make a big difference, especially for elderly neighbors or those recovering from illness.

## THE RIPPLE EFFECT OF HELPING WITH CHORES

The afternoon spent restoring Mrs. Keller's garden became the beginning of an unexpected friendship. In the days that followed, Lindsay and Mrs. Keller found themselves exchanging friendly greetings each morning, and Mrs. Keller often invited Lindsay to sit with her on the porch for tea or left her small homemade treats as a quiet thank-you. What started as help with a single task slowly grew into a meaningful connection rooted in trust and care.

Simple acts of assistance often carry more weight than we realize. When someone is overwhelmed, help with everyday chores offers more than physical relief. It communicates compassion, dignity, and support. In this case, sharing the work not only eased Mrs. Keller's burden but also created a lasting bond, reminding both the older woman and Lindsay that kindness has the power to change daily life in ways that extend far beyond a com

## CHAPTER 21

# *Mentoring*

As a new college graduate with a degree in marketing, Riley was both excited and nervous to attend a networking gathering of industry professionals at her local community center. Clutching her notes and adjusting her blazer as she entered the room, she searched for a familiar face in the crowded space. Although she'd decided to attend the event to explore job opportunities, she felt lost, unsure of how to approach someone she didn't know and begin a conversation.

I was seated by the coffee stand when Riley approached me and introduced herself, her voice carrying both strength and apprehension. She told me her name and expressed her desire to learn more about breaking into the marketing industry. Her willingness to take a risk captured my attention, and I slipped my phone into my pocket, smiled at her, and said, "I'd be happy to help you with any marketing career advice you need, Riley."

She spent the next twenty minutes sharing her background with me. She told me she loved designing creative campaigns and storytelling, yet felt it was impossible for new grads to enter the marketing industry. She'd submitted numerous job applications and hadn't received a single response and had no idea what she was doing wrong.

"Your dedication to the marketing field is evident," I told her, "and that already puts you on the right path. I'd love to work together to enhance your approach. I can help you improve your résumé, practice effective interviewing techniques, and connect you with some professionals in the field. How does that sound?"

That was the beginning of a rewarding mentorship experience for both of us. Focusing on a few clear, achievable goals, I first identified ways Riley could highlight her internship and volunteer experience in her résumé. Then we conducted mock interviews to help her gain confidence for the interviewing process. I also connected her with several industry professionals to help her expand her network. Riley's confidence grew after each mentoring session. She began submitting applications with a strong sense of purpose, using her unique strengths and genuine passion to make her materials stand out.

During one of our sessions, Riley confided that she struggled with imposter syndrome and often doubted her abilities. I shared my own experiences with self-doubt and told her, "Everyone experiences this at some point. The path to success isn't about perfection—it's about tracking your progress. You belong in this space, and your commitment to excellence will reaffirm your worth to yourself."

After several months of searching, Riley secured her first interview at a mid-sized marketing agency. The evening before, she called me to express her nerves about the interview. I reassured her, "Your authentic self will shine through. You're prepared."

The next day, she called me again—this time with joy in her voice. She'd been offered the position, and the interview team expressed how much they appreciated her creative thinking and genuine enthusiasm. Riley had taken the guidance I'd offered and transformed it into her own personal triumph. She excelled in her new role, delivering innovative solutions and showing unwavering commitment to her work. After just one year, she was promoted to project manager. She'd also begun mentoring a younger colleague. "I want to help her the way you helped me," she explained.

## THE POWER OF MENTORING

Mentorship involves more than sharing information; it requires believing in another person's future success while helping them develop self-belief. A mentor offers guidance and support through challenging times and moments of triumph, providing fresh perspectives and gentle protection from missteps. Through the relationship, the mentee builds confidence and gains access to new possibilities they may not have discovered on their own. Over time, mentorship becomes a steady source of encouragement that empowers growth, resilience, and independence.

## PRACTICAL WAYS TO BE A MENTOR

- **Listen Actively:** Begin by understanding your mentee's goals, challenges, and aspirations. Show genuine interest and ask leading questions.

- **Share Your Own Story:** Personal experiences, including both successes and failures, provide valuable lessons and inspiration.
- **Assist in Setting Actionable Goals:** Help your mentee break down their objectives into achievable steps, offering guidance and accountability.
- **Provide Resources:** Share books, articles, tools, or contacts that can support their growth.
- **Encourage Resilience:** Help them navigate setbacks by reframing challenges as opportunities for growth.
- **Celebrate Wins:** Acknowledge their achievements, no matter how small, to help build their confidence.
- **Advocate for Their Independence:** Empower them to start making their own decisions and trusting their abilities.

## THE RIPPLE EFFECT OF MENTORING

Your investment in someone else's development will produce advantages that extend beyond their own individual growth to affect others they'll support in the future. Mentoring creates a chain of empowerment that establishes a tradition of leadership and compassion. The process of mentoring develops self-assurance while people grow both personally and professionally.

When you take the time to mentor another person, you can achieve a feeling of accomplishment while simultaneously strengthening your own life journey. The practice of sharing wisdom leads to an increase in its total value. A society that provides guidance to its members will help replace the current—and often damaging—culture of competitive individualism with a collaborative, healthy environment. As we dedicate ourselves to helping each other succeed, the result will be a network of support that generates new possibilities and positive expectations.

## CHAPTER 22

# *Showing Up*

Emi had spent a full twelve months preparing for her debut solo violin performance. At age fourteen, she dedicated countless hours to practicing, often alone in her room, striving for artistic perfection. Music was her passion, yet it came with a challenge: Emi suffered from severe performance anxiety.

Her parents, who worked demanding full-time jobs, supported her in spirit but rarely attended her performances. Emi assumed this recital would be no different. As the date approached, she tried to hide her disappointment, telling herself it was fine. She'd tell them all about it after the concert, just like she always did.

One afternoon, Emi mentioned her upcoming performance to her neighbor, Mrs. Carter, who had a deep appreciation for classical music. Mrs. Carter's face brightened, and she told Emi she'd love to see her perform live.

When the recital day arrived, Emi stood backstage with her violin, her nerves so intense she could feel the vibrations in her strings. She peeked through the curtain and there, sitting in the third row of the audience, was Mrs. Carter, waving at Emi with a warm smile and wearing a colorful scarf. Knowing Mrs. Carter had shown up for her brought Emi a sense of peace and joy. Someone had come just for her! That realization gave her the strength to walk onto the stage. And when she did, she received another surprise: Her parents were seated in the front row, which was all it took to turn Emi's nervousness into excitement.

As the lights illuminated her, Emi took a deep breath and began to play. Violin music filled the room with its enchanting sound as Emi quickly found her rhythm and poured her whole heart into the performance. When she finished, the audience erupted in applause, with Mrs. Carter and her parents clapping and cheering louder than anyone.

Afterward, Emi found Mrs. Carter in the crowd and thanked her for attending the performance. Mrs. Carter smiled broadly and said, "Your performance was outstanding. You have a natural talent, and I am so proud to have watched you perform." And then Emi spotted her parents. She ran to them and hugged them tightly, thanking them and telling them how much she loved them. Her performance anxiety was long forgotten—people who cared had shown up for her, further erasing all of her pre-performance doubt and anxiety.

## THE POWER OF SHOWING UP

Showing up for someone's event may seem small, but it carries tremendous weight. Your presence communicates, "You matter, and what you're doing matters." For someone who has worked hard, felt nervous, or wondered if anyone even cares, seeing a familiar face in the crowd can be the encouragement they desperately need.

The power of attending is about the message your presence sends: *You are valued. You are supported. You are worth showing up for.* By simply being there, you offer affirmation, connection, and encouragement that often lasts far beyond the moment itself.

## PRACTICAL WAYS TO SHOW UP

- **Be Fully Present:** Put away your phone, engage with the moment, and show genuine interest.

- **Invite Others:** Rally additional support by bringing friends or family to cheer them on.
- **Celebrate Their Efforts:** Offer specific compliments about what impressed you, which shows that you were truly paying attention.
- **Document the Moment:** Take photos or videos (if appropriate) and share them as a keepsake.
- **Follow Up:** After the event, check in to reflect on their experience and celebrate their success.

## THE RIPPLE EFFECT OF SHOWING UP

Showing up for someone may seem small, but it creates ripples that can transform their life. Presence validates their efforts, strengthens confidence, and reminds them that their gifts deserve to be seen. As people feel supported, they step into bigger opportunities, grow as leaders, and begin supporting others in return.

Communities become stronger when people show up for one another. A simple act of attendance can turn an ordinary event into a moment of connection, trust, and belonging—one that continues to shape a person long after the applause fades.

## CHAPTER 23

# *Babysitting*

Britt was a single mother raising her two children, Avery and Jackson, who were four and seven years old. Her demanding work schedule combined with her children's nonstop energy drained every ounce of her strength. Matters became even more challenging when Britt's mother—who often took care of the kids—underwent surgery, leaving her unable to help.

On top of everything, Britt had an upcoming job interview for a promotion—an opportunity that could significantly improve her family's future. The interview was scheduled for a weekday evening, and finding child-care on such short notice felt impossible.

During a brief hallway encounter in their apartment building, Britt confided her childcare struggle to Addie, a college student who babysat for extra income. Without hesitation, Addie offered to watch Avery and Jackson. She greeted the children warmly, showing them the snacks, toys, and books she had gathered from a friend.

Addie began the evening by building Legos with Jackson, then read a storybook to Avery using a variety of comedic voices. Later, she helped them make mini pizzas with prepped toppings. Laughter filled the room as the children decorated their pizzas with creative arrangements of cheese and pepperoni.

After dinner, Addie constructed a cozy blanket fort in the living room. She, Avery, and Jackson climbed inside with flashlights to share funny stories and perform shadow puppet shows. By bedtime, the children were calm, happy, and ready for sleep. Addie tucked them in with their favorite stuffed animals, and they drifted peacefully off to sleep.

When Britt returned home, she found Addie tidying up after the pizza party, while Avery and Jackson slept soundly in their beds. Tears filled Britt's eyes as she expressed her heartfelt gratitude. Addie simply waved it off, saying, "Your children are wonderful. I had a fun time with them!"

## THE POWER OF BABYSITTING

Babysitting may feel like a small favor, but its impact

often runs much deeper. Offering care for someone else's children creates space for parents or guardians to rest, focus, and tend to parts of their lives that are often placed on hold. That time might be used to pursue work opportunities, care for their mental and emotional well-being, or simply catch up on much-needed sleep. Knowing their children are safe and cared for brings a sense of relief that cannot be overstated. When someone steps in with willingness and trust, it reminds parents that they are not meant to carry everything alone and that shared responsibility strengthens both families and communities.

## PRACTICAL WAYS TO OFFER BABYSITTING SUPPORT

- **Be Proactive:** If you know someone who might need a break, offer your help before they even have a chance to ask.
- **Create a Fun Plan:** Prepare activities or games that will keep the children engaged and happy.
- **Communicate Clearly:** Make sure to ask about any allergies, routines, or special needs the children might have.
- **Check In:** Send a quick update during the

babysitting session to reassure the parent that everything is going well.

- **Make It Easy:** Offer flexible times and locations to accommodate the parent's schedule.

## THE RIPPLE EFFECT OF BABYSITTING

The gift of childcare, even for just a few hours, produces effects that extend beyond the babysitting session. Getting help with childcare encourages families to develop trust while connecting communities and providing parents with reassurance about their support network. Parents who receive help develop better family bonds, and their work performance improves as well because of increased peace of mind, knowing that their children are safe.

Those caring for the children learn to be more patient and increase their compassion while taking on greater responsibility and serving their community. Babysitters learn vital life skills through their work, including problem-solving strategies and effective communication techniques. The children in their care find consistency and joy through their caregiver's playful behavior and loving attitude. And everyone involved—parent, babysitter, and child—feels valued and supported.

## CHAPTER 24

# *Connection*

Susan always started her day by walking to her job, wearing headphones to help block out the sounds of the city and give her a little peace before beginning her workday. She preferred to avoid distractions, looking straight ahead while keeping her walking speed constant, focusing on everything awaiting her at work.

Ben was a homeless man who lived on a corner near the neighborhood bakery, and Susan encountered him every day on her morning commute. He always greeted her with a happy "Good morning!" even though she never responded to him. At most, she'd give him a brief nod as she briskly walked by.

One day, Susan departed from her house earlier than usual. Noticing that Ben was already occupying his regular spot near the bakery, she decided to use her extra time to stop and talk to the homeless man instead of rushing by him. The combination of his friendly smile and familiar face prompted her to take off her headphones, and they began an actual conversation for the first time.

Ben revealed to Susan that he'd served in the military before working as an auto mechanic. As Ben shared about his military experiences and described his lost comrades and his post-military mental health battles, Susan realized how much she'd been ignoring the people who lived right around her while rushing through her daily routine. She wondered what other things she had missed.

Their brief encounter turned into extended conversations. Susan returned to talk with Ben every couple of days after that first meeting. They discussed a wide range of topics—urban life, the military, music, the weather. Susan began to look forward to their conversations. She also began bringing food to Ben on her way home from work. The food brought him joy, but he told her he valued their time together more than any meal.

The passing weeks brought about a transformation in Susan's personality. She started walking at a slower pace while observing and appreciating her surroundings, and she developed new social connections that reawakened a sense of ease and openness she hadn't felt in years. Susan's new mentality helped Ben too. He was used to people ignoring him and acting like he wasn't there, and Susan's actions helped him realize he was a person of value who was worth befriending.

A single morning greeting between two people from very different worlds developed into a friendly bond that brought unexpected positive change to them both.

## THE POWER OF CONNECTION

Taking the time to focus on others and connect with them can be the start of genuine friendships, which make everyone feel valued. Intentional acknowledgment and conversation can have a life-changing impact on people who experience loneliness and social isolation. Personal connection with another human being enables them to build social bonds with others while restoring their happiness as they realize they have people who value and care about them.

## PRACTICAL WAYS TO CONNECT

- **Start Small:** A simple wave or a short visit can open the door to a deeper connection.
- **Be Consistent:** Regular visits, even if they're brief, show that you care and give both people something to look forward to.
- **Share Activities:** Engage in hobbies or pastimes together—gardening, cooking, even watching a favorite TV show.
- **Be a Listener:** Sometimes the best gift you can give is a listening ear, free of judgment or distraction.
- **Involve Them:** Invite people who are lonely to outings or gatherings, helping them feel more included in the broader community.

## THE RIPPLE EFFECT OF CONNECTION

When Susan took time out of her morning commute and spoke with Ben, a homeless veteran she encountered daily, she recognized him as a fellow human while acknowledging that his life held value. Their initial casual conversation developed into a consistent connection. The food that Susan delivered to Ben served as more than sustenance—it carried a message of respect and compassion. And Ben wasn't the only one who benefited from their connection—Susan learned how to remove her headphones, slow down, look around, and truly experience the world around her that she'd previously been ignoring. Even brief encounters can produce substantial effects—that's the power of connection.

## CHAPTER 25

# *Dog Walking*

MRS. THOMPSON, a retired teacher, had lived in her home for forty years. As her arthritis progressed, everyday tasks had become increasingly difficult. Her biggest concern was her four-year-old golden retriever, Teddy, an energetic dog with a high need for long walks, squirrel chases, and constant neighborhood exploration. Sadly, Mrs. Thompson's declining health made it hard for her to keep up with him.

Patti, a graduate student, had recently moved in next door to Mrs. Thompson. She loved animals but couldn't own a pet due to her hectic academic life and limited space. Seeing Teddy stare longingly out the window made her feel sad because she knew he wanted to be outside.

One day, Patti noticed Mrs. Thompson struggling with Teddy's leash. Patti approached the older woman with a warm smile and said, "Teddy seems like such a sweet dog. I love dogs, but I can't have one right now. Would you allow me to take Teddy for walks?" Mrs. Thompson gratefully accepted Patti's offer, relieved to know Teddy would finally be able to receive the exercise he needed.

Patti began taking Teddy on daily walks, and the simple favor soon grew into a special routine. Teddy showed his excitement by bounding around joyfully, while Patti enjoyed watching him greet every dog and owner they encountered. Knowing that Teddy was getting proper care also brought immense comfort to Mrs. Thompson. She loved hearing Patti's stories about their walks, and the photos of Teddy that Patti texted her from their outings helped her feel like she was right there with them.

Over time, the women built a strong bond that extended beyond dog walking. After her walks with Teddy, Patti often stayed and had tea with Mrs. Thompson, and they talked about everything from the older woman's teaching days to the younger woman's grad school stories.

Mrs. Thompson even became a source of guidance for Patti as she navigated academic pressures and impending career decisions.

When Patti noticed that Mrs. Thompson's garden had become overgrown, she offered to help. She gathered several friends to clean up the yard and plant new flowers while Teddy happily supervised, his tail wagging throughout the entire project. What started as a dog-walking favor had turned into a rewarding friendship—for all three of them.

## THE POWER OF DOG WALKING

Taking on the task of dog walking for owners who need assistance—whether they're physically unable or too busy—meets both the pet's and the human's needs. The combination of exercise and social interaction brings happiness to dogs like Teddy, while their owners experience peace of mind because their pets are receiving proper care. Dog walking also enables people to establish bonds with their neighbors, which strengthens their community ties. Plus, it's fun and good exercise for the person taking the dog on a walk!

## PRACTICAL WAYS TO PROVIDE DOG-WALKING ASSISTANCE

- **Start Small:** Offer to walk a neighbor's or a shelter's dog once a week, or whenever you have spare time.
- **Be Consistent:** Create a regular schedule so the pet and owner can consistently rely on you.
- **Communicate Clearly:** Ask about the dog's preferences, health needs, and temperament before taking them out.
- **Engage with the Pet:** Play with the dog or explore new routes to make the walks even more enjoyable.
- **Spread the Word:** Encourage others in your community to offer similar help, especially to elderly or busy neighbors.

## THE RIPPLE EFFECT OF DOG WALKING

Patti's generous nature inspired others in the neighborhood to offer their own help when they saw her out walking Teddy. Neighbors started checking on Mrs. Thompson—and other elderly people on the street—and offered to help her with grocery shopping and basic home upkeep. Patti also received several positive advantages that she hadn't been expecting. Taking Teddy for daily walks helped her control the stress of grad school while her growing friendship with Mrs. Thompson—and eventually other neighbors—helped her feel comfortable in her new residential area.

The practice of showing love through small actions, such as taking a neighbor's dog for a walk, helps develop trust and empathy and creates deep human relationships—and connections with furry friends. Dogs owners receive both physical relief and emotional peace knowing that their pets are receiving proper care and attention. And the dog walkers feel accomplished, gain mental clarity, and experience emotional satisfaction through their work. Dog walking is also good for the community, as it helps to create an atmosphere where residents watch out for one another while allowing animals to serve as social bridges that connect people who might not otherwise interact.

CHAPTER 26

# *Letter Writing*

Aliyah was spending a quiet Saturday afternoon going through the contents of some shoeboxes that hadn't been touched in at least a decade. The shoeboxes contained various items including outdated greeting cards, used tickets, and faded photographs. In one box, a small envelope with her father's handwriting caught her attention. She pulled it out, opened the envelope, and took a deep breath before she started reading the letter. The message inside revealed something she'd been longing to hear:

My dear Aliyah,

If you're reading this, I want you to know how deeply proud I am of you. Life will get heavy sometimes, but you are stronger than you realize. Don't rush through the world—slow down and let the people you love know what they mean to you. My greatest joy has always been being your father.

With all my love,
Dad

Aliyah started crying before she even got to the end of the letter. The words felt like they were crossing time—reaching into her present life, holding her close in a way she hadn't felt in years. And the simple but profound words from her father brought about a transformation within her, telling her what she had always needed to know.

Aliyah hadn't realized how a single sheet of paper could contain such power. A few handwritten lines from her father possessed the ability to provide comfort and direction, even though he was no longer living. She had so much she wanted to share with her own children, and now she was inspired to write these things down. Pulling out a brand-new notebook and a pen, Aliyah started writing letters to her children, imagining a future time when they would need her words of encouragement and reassurance and love.

In each letter, Aliyah documented that child's positive qualities, talked about their aspirations, and gave advice and encouragement about how to handle life's difficulties. She also wrote down all the memories that she wanted her children to remember forever. When she finished, she placed each letter in an envelope, sealed it, and wrote the recipient's name on the front. Then she added the letters to her own shoebox of memories.

## THE POWER OF LETTER WRITING

A handwritten note may be just words written on paper, but it's so much more than that because it represents the genuine emotions and heart of the writer. People love to read letters that demonstrate their importance to others. The notes provide them with comfort and help them remember that they are valued.

Physical handwritten letters have more sentimental value than digital messages because they're tangible items that the recipients can save and look at again and again. People can find encouragement in these letters during challenging times, as they're a reminder that authentic kindness continues to exist in this world. Writing a letter takes minimal time, yet its message can live on for generations.

## PRACTICAL WAYS TO WRITE LETTERS

- **Choose Your Recipient:** Think of someone who might need a word of encouragement, an expression of gratitude, or simply a reminder that they're appreciated.
- **Keep It Personal:** Mention specific memories, qualities, or things the recipient has done that made a difference.
- **Be Genuine:** Write from the heart—your sincerity will matter more than perfect wording.
- **Add a Personal Touch:** Include a favorite quote, a doodle, or even a small keepsake like a pressed flower or photo.
- **Deliver Thoughtfully:** Mailing your note can make it feel extra special, but handing it to someone personally can also create a beautiful, shared moment.

## THE RIPPLE EFFECT OF LETTER WRITING

Finding a lost letter from her deceased father marked the start of Aliyah's new habit of sharing her love through letter writing. With the realization that written words survive beyond the time we exist in this world, Aliyah began writing notes more frequently to her children, hiding encouraging messages inside their lunch boxes and even sending letters through mail for no specific reason.

Reading letters written to us can bring comfort while motivating us to share our own thoughts and feelings through the written word. Letter writing connects us with others, helps us express what might be hard to say in person, and gives the recipients some of the most precious items anyone could possess.

CHAPTER 27

# *Reading Together*

TEN-YEAR-OLD KENNEDY spent most of her summer break glued to her tablet, playing games and watching videos while her required summer reading list collected dust on her dresser. With school only a few weeks away, she still hadn't finished a single book and didn't feel particularly motivated to start.

Every Friday, Kennedy's mom took her to visit her grandmother, Grandma Rose, who lived in a cheerful but quiet nursing home. Kennedy cared about her grandma, but she often found the visits dull, especially when the adults drifted into long, boring conversations. She usually sat in the corner with her tablet, counting down the minutes until it was time to go.

One warm afternoon, Grandma Rose noticed

Kennedy scrolling aimlessly and gently reminded her, "Summer's almost over, sweetheart. How's that reading list coming along?"

Kennedy shrugged. "It's boring."

Grandma Rose smiled knowingly. "I noticed you brought one of your books. Why don't you read something out loud to me? Stories feel different when they're shared."

With nothing else to do, Kennedy sighed, opened the book, and began to read. Her voice was quiet at first, but Grandma Rose leaned in, listening with full attention. A few minutes later, another resident rolled her wheelchair closer. Then another shuffled in with his walker. Soon, an entire semicircle of residents had gathered, drawn by Kennedy's expressive voice and the nostalgia of story time, something many of them hadn't experienced in years.

Kennedy looked up, startled by her growing audience. "You all want to listen?" she asked in disbelief.

"Of course we do," one gentleman said, chuckling. "It's been ages since someone read to us."

Feeling a little shy but oddly proud, Kennedy continued. As the chapters unfolded, her confidence grew. She used different voices for characters, paused for dramatic effect, and even made the group laugh during funny scenes. By the time she finished reading the first chapter, the residents applauded warmly.

"Same time next week?" a woman asked with hopeful eyes.

Kennedy grinned. "Yeah … I think so."

And just like that, "Story Time with Kennedy" became a weekly event at the nursing home. She finished her summer reading faster than ever, and once the schoolbooks were done, she brought other stories—mysteries, fairy tales, funny chapter books. The residents began saving her a special seat in the center of their lounge, and Grandma Rose watched proudly as her shy granddaughter became the heart of their Friday afternoons. And what had once felt like a boring obligation turned into one of Kennedy's favorite parts of the week.

## THE POWER OF READING TOGETHER

Reading aloud creates a common experience that brings people together. Children who are read aloud to develop their creative thinking and language abilities and gain a greater capacity to understand different perspectives. Reading aloud to seniors helps them sharpen their cognitive skills and maintain good mental health while fighting loneliness and giving them a sense of meaning.

Groups that read together become united with listening, laughter, and reflection as the stories shared come to life. Having different age groups read together is especially effective for uniting communities, with stronger relationships being built as people share their own life experience and learn from each other.

## PRACTICAL WAYS TO START READING TOGETHER

- **Choose the Right Setting:** Find a cozy, quiet space where everyone feels comfortable and free from distractions.
- **Pick Engaging Books:** Select stories that match the interests and reading levels of everyone involved—adventure tales, classics, and humorous titles all work wonderfully.
- **Take Turns Reading:** Alternate readers to make the experience more interactive and empowering for all participants.

- **Discuss the Story:** Pause to share thoughts about the characters, themes, or lessons. These conversations help to deepen understanding and connection.
- **Make It a Routine:** Schedule regular reading times—weekly or daily—to build anticipation and strengthen the reading bonds.

## THE RIPPLE EFFECT OF READING TOGETHER

Kennedy walked into her grandmother's nursing home each week expecting to be bored, but reading aloud transformed her visits into something she genuinely looked forward to. The residents began eagerly anticipating her stories, and Kennedy discovered confidence, purpose, and a love of reading she didn't know she had.

What started as a reluctant attempt to finish a summer assignment became a cherished tradition that brought joy to both a little girl and a room full of elders, proving that even the smallest shared moments—like half an hour of reading together—can create ripples of connection that brighten many lives.

CHAPTER 28

# *Meal Trains*

AFTER GIVING BIRTH to her fourth child, Erica found herself experiencing unexpected and overwhelming stress. Her husband had to return to work almost immediately, leaving her to juggle a newborn, three young kids, sleepless nights, and a schedule that never seemed to slow down, along with a house that never seemed to stay clean and organized. Even the simplest tasks—like figuring out what to have for dinner—felt impossible.

When a close friend observed Erica's overwhelming situation, she decided to take immediate action. She immediately set up a meal train, which she shared with all of their mutual friends, church members, and neighbors. Right away, fourteen people signed up to provide dinners for Erica's family for the next two weeks. Each day, a different volunteer brought Erica's family a hot meal, and the family enjoyed a variety of casseroles, soups, and slow-cooker dishes as well as fresh salads, homemade breads, and sweet treats. The meal deliveries included hugs, words of encouragement, and brief but important conversations, which assured Erica that she had people who cared about her during this challenging season of life.

Erica was also able to experience her first moments of relaxation since the baby had come home and her husband had returned to work. The meal train eliminated her need to plan, grocery shop, and cook during those extremely tiring days. She spent this time doing the important work of resting and bonding with her newborn, and also creating special memories with her other three children. A system of support and kindness, organized in the form of a friend's meal train, helped turn Erica's overwhelming stress into a manageable schedule, strengthening her, her family, and her friendships.

## THE POWER OF MEAL TRAINS

Since ancient times, human beings have established relationships through the practice of sharing food with others. Providing nourishment for others also fulfills the fundamental human requirement for social connection and caring for each other. The meal train service provided Erica with benefits that went beyond food delivery. The dinner deliveries brought her emotional support and comfort while showing her that multiple people loved her. Multiple friends from various parts of her life united to provide support during her challenging time.

When you prepare someone a meal and deliver it, they understand their value to you. The practice of delivering food to others creates opportunities for friendship while building stronger community bonds and demonstrates that small gestures of kindness can create substantial comfort during both stressful and joyful times.

## PRACTICAL WAYS TO HELP WITH MEAL TRAINS

- **Organize a Meal Schedule:** A shared schedule helps ensure meals are provided consistently without overwhelming any one person.
- **Use Techology to Invite Others:** Share the meal train through social media, group chats, or neighborhood apps to invite friends, coworkers, and community members to participate. This

allows many people to contribute in small ways and ensures ongoing support.

- **Keep Meals Simple and Thoughtful:** Choose easy, comforting dishes that reheat well, like casseroles, soups, or freezer-ready meals. Simple food can be deeply meaningful when it removes the stress of daily cooking.
- **Coordinate Preferences and Needs:** Communicate about dietary restrictions, allergies, or favorite foods. Thoughtful planning ensures meals are helpful, not burdensome.
- **Deliver with Care:** Drop off meals at an agreed-upon time and respect the family's or individual's need for rest or privacy. A kind note left with the meal can offer encouragement without requiring conversation.
- **Encourage Ongoing Participation:** Remind participants that there are many ways to provide a meal. Store-bought meals, delivery services, or gift cards are just as valuable as home-cooked dishes.

## THE RIPPLE EFFECT OF MEAL TRAINS

Erica's meal train provided her with more than nightly dinners—it showed her that people were there to support her during a challenging time. The meals she received brought her comfort and encouragement while giving her a bit of breathing room in her overwhelming schedule. And the support she received helped transform her life. Later on, she started noticing others—new mothers, sick friends, struggling neighbors—who also might benefit from being the recipient of a meal train.

The act of scheduling dinner deliveries for one individual can lead to a widespread community effort to prepare and deliver meals to those in need of them. The meal train recipients receive not only nourishment from the food delivered, but the gift of genuine kindness and compassion—and then once they're in a position to help, they pass that on to others.

## CHAPTER 29

# *Celebrating Milestones*

OLIVIA HAD BEEN a steady presence in her office for fifteen years. She worked as the team's accountant, providing dependable service, dedicated effort, and steady support to her colleagues. Despite her long tenure at the company, Olivia's reserved nature often resulted in her blending into the background during social events.

One day, her coworker Becca overheard Olivia mention that she would soon be celebrating her fiftieth birthday. This simple remark left a lasting impression on Becca, who felt the milestone deserved recognition. When she found out that Olivia hadn't planned any type of celebration, Becca gathered several coworkers to propose throwing a surprise birthday party for their quiet colleague. Some team members hesitated, unsure whether Olivia, who avoided drawing attention to herself, would appreciate such a gesture. But Becca remained firm: *Everyone* deserved to be celebrated during important life events, and Olivia's quiet nature did not mean she wouldn't appreciate and enjoy the party.

Eventually, the team agreed with Becca's plan and divided up the responsibilities. They chose decorations, prepared food, and selected a meaningful gift. Becca took on the special task of collecting stories and written messages from coworkers to create a physical scrapbook that would show Olivia just how much she meant to the team.

Olivia's birthday began like any other day in the office. She placed her coffee mug on her desk and started her morning tasks. Then Becca asked her to join her in the conference room to discuss a budget matter. When Olivia walked in, she was greeted by balloons and a large banner that read "Happy 50th, Olivia!" The table was decorated with her favorite sunflowers, and a birthday cake with the message "50 Years of Brilliance" sat proudly in the center. As the team broke into applause, Olivia froze for a moment, tears welling up in her eyes. Then she asked whether they had truly organized all of this for her birthday. Becca stepped forward and said warmly,

"Your dedication to our team has been so valuable, and we wanted to honor you on your special day."

The celebration unfolded with shared stories, laughter, and a meal enjoyed together. Olivia opened up about her early days at the company, telling stories about the things she'd accomplished as well as the challenges she'd faced over the years. Her coworkers shared memories of how Olivia consistently helped others, remembered their coffee preferences, and supported them in quiet but meaningful ways. The scrapbook turned out to be the highlight of the event. Filled with heartfelt messages praising Olivia's kindness, her professionalism, and her ability to brighten everyone's day, it moved Olivia deeply. Her face glowed with happiness as she read each page, tears streaming down her cheeks. And she told the group she never imagined people in the office felt this way about her.

The team's effort to surprise Olivia created not just a birthday milestone celebration but a moment of recognition she had long deserved. Their thoughtful preparations—decorating the room, preparing the food, selecting gifts, crafting the scrapbook—came together to create a truly memorable and meaningful experience for a dedicated coworker and friend.

## THE POWER OF CELEBRATING MILESTONES

The act of celebrating another person's birthday, achievement, or another type of personal milestone represents more than a nice gesture—it demonstrates that they're important to us. We build stronger relationships with one another when we recognize their important life events. The celebration demonstrates that someone's achievement—no matter how small—is worthy of recognition. The surprise party Olivia received showed her that she was valuable to others at her company. Over time, the organization adopted regular practices to celebrate birthdays, personal achievements, and professional milestones, fostering a year marked by increased morale, stronger teamwork, and a more connected and supportive environment for everyone.

People gain awareness of their personal value when others recognize their birthdays, their achievements, and other milestones in their lives. The practice of celebration through parties, gifts, cards, and joyful gatherings creates a sense of happiness and connection for both the person being celebrated and the ones putting on the celebration.

## PRACTICAL WAYS TO CELEBRATE MILESTONES

- **Know Their Preferences:** Consider what kind of celebration would make them most comfortable—a big party, a small gathering, a heartfelt note, a shared meal.
- **Be Thoughtful:** Personalize the gesture with things they love—favorite colors, foods, music, or flowers.
- **Include Others:** Invite people who have played a role in their story—coworkers, friends, or family.
- **Capture the Memories:** Create a keepsake such as a photo album, scrapbook, or video to commemorate the occasion.
- **Focus on Them:** Let the celebration reflect their personality, achievements, and journey. Make it about who they are, not just what they've done.

## THE RIPPLE EFFECT OF CELEBRATING MILESTONES

The surprise birthday party Olivia received showed her that her value came from who she was as a person rather than what she'd achieved at work. The team's kindness boosted her self-assurance and happiness, proving that even a quiet, unassuming presence can have a profound effect on others. The celebration brought positive changes to the entire workplace environment and led to some new office traditions, which included birthday parties, team celebrations, and random positive feedback sessions. The dedication to regular recognition of employees established a supportive environment that led to increased trust, better morale, and deeper friendships.

People naturally are motivated to express appreciation for their colleagues when their workplace environment promotes celebrating others. Special events in work environments and communities enable people to build strong social bonds as they establish deeper interpersonal connections. Celebrating milestones is an excellent way to show honor and appreciation for individuals while strengthening the entire group.

CHAPTER 30

# *Phone Calls*

Hannah sat by her window, looking out at the street below. Her move to a new city six months earlier had proven to be far more challenging than she'd expected. The nonstop noise only intensified her feelings of isolation. She longed for the comfort of her family, her friends, and the familiar sense of home she'd left behind. That afternoon as she sat by the window, she was wondering if anyone from back home still thought about her.

At that very moment, her phone rang. The call was from her college friend Kylie. "Hi, Hannah! I've been thinking about you. How have you been?"

The sound of Kylie's voice made Hannah's throat tighten. She'd been deep in her own pity party, telling herself that everyone from her old life had forgotten her.

At first, she struggled to respond, unsure of what to say. But Kylie's warm, sincere tone helped her to open up, and soon Hannah found herself sharing her true feelings.

Kylie listened attentively, offering silence when Hannah needed space to speak. When the call ended, Hannah felt as though a heavy weight had been lifted. That simple phone call from her college roommate reminded her that she was not alone—there were people in her life who cared about her and would reach out.

That one call sparked a transformation. Feeling supported, Hannah reached out to a colleague for coffee and began to participate in a few local activities, including a neighborhood book club, a weekend walking group, and community events she had previously scrolled past without a second thought. Each small step helped her feel more connected and less alone. Over time, she built a solid social network within her community. That brief call from Kylie created a lasting shift in Hannah's life, giving her the confidence to put down roots and truly feel at home in a new environment.

Hannah's story shows how something as simple as a quick phone call can deeply impact someone who's desperate for connection. When we take the time to reach out, we help others feel seen, valued, and supported. Conversation offers clarity and reassurance, giving people the strength to move forward. For the caller, the time investment is minimal; for the recipient, it can be life-changing.

In a fast-paced society that's often devoid of personal connections, people need genuine communication more than ever. Social media posts and text messages can keep us informed, but they often fail to create the emotional depth that a phone conversation offers. The immediate and personal nature of a phone call—and especially a FaceTime call—allows people to connect on a deeper level, laughing and even crying together as they form bonds that remain strong regardless of physical distance.

## THE POWER OF PHONE CALLS

Phone conversations create strong emotional responses, which helps people to bond and grow their relationships. A phone call enables us to provide more than just words—it establishes a physical connection with the person on the other end of the call. People who hear familiar voices experience higher levels of security, which leads to reduced stress and increased happiness.

When we talk on the phone with another person, we're sharing life experiences with each other, listening to each other, and forming lasting memories. And phone calls don't require complicated setups or exact timing. A casual call is a quick but effective way to show someone else our support and, like Kylie did with Hannah, let another person know we're thinking about them and we care about them.

## PRACTICAL WAYS TO CONNECT THROUGH PHONE CALLS

- **Set a Reminder:** Life gets busy, and it's easy to forget to check in with loved ones. Set a reminder on your phone or calendar to call a friend or family member regularly.
- **Be Intentional:** When you call, focus on the other person. Ask meaningful questions and actively listen to their responses. Avoid multitasking during the conversation.
- **Reach Out Randomly:** Sometimes, an unexpected call can be the brightest spot in someone's day. Trust your instincts—if someone crosses your mind, take it as a sign to check in.

- **Rely on Technology:** Consider video calling for a more personal touch. Seeing the other person's face can really enhance your connection.

## THE RIPPLE EFFECT OF PHONE CALLS

The phone call Hannah received brought back her sense of hope and belonging at a time in her life when she was feeling disconnected from others. People who are experiencing loneliness are boosted by something as small as a phone call, which shows them that others value them. Kylie dedicated a few minutes of her day to show Hannah kindness, which deepened their friendship and kept them connected despite living in two different places.

Our ability to empathize with others and maintain strong relationships grows through our ongoing efforts to stay connected. One phone call can lead to many—and eventual FaceTime chats and personal visits. People who receive support tend to pass that support to others, which produces a chain reaction of positive social connections.

## CHAPTER 31

# *Kind Words*

As a young artist, Liam was encountering professional barriers in his career pursuits. His field had reached an extremely competitive state, and his creative energy had started to fade as galleries and clients kept rejecting his work. Self-doubt began to consume him, and he began to doubt his abilities, which resulted in him beginning to lose his passion for art. After he received his fourth gallery rejection in a row, Liam toyed with the idea of fully giving up on his artistic dreams and pursuing a new career.

Not quite ready to throw in the towel, Liam decided to try one last thing. He uploaded a new piece of artwork, a painting of his childhood home, and shared it on Instagram, Behance, and ArtStation. He had no expectations and figured he had nothing to lose. However, someone who saw and was moved by the beauty of Liam's painting posted a comment, observing that the piece displayed both artistic beauty and strong emotional intensity. The authentic praise and positive feedback from a stranger who had stumbled across his painting online gave Liam the power to keep going with his art.

Some words of kindness posted online triggered an instant boost of motivation, and Liam's passion for art was quickly rekindled. The authenticity of the comment resulted in him regaining his drive. Another poster revealed their own experiences with rejection and perseverance and described how this resulted in a path to success. The supportive words he read helped Liam regain his confidence, which led him to discover renewed inspiration and fresh artistic collaborations that eventually brought him surprising career breakthroughs. And it all began because someone had taken the time to share some kind words.

## THE POWER OF KIND WORDS

Kind words have the ability to bring new life to people who feel discouraged or exhausted. The value of these words far exceeds their cost, which is zero. A few words of encouragement during times of uncertainty or challenges can be exactly what someone needs to renew their determination and continue their journey. Words of kindness create more than comfort—they establish hope in people's lives as they transform into confidence and courage and strength. Through well-chosen words, we possess the ability to create positive change, which leads to healing and transformation in our world.

We face a daily decision: use our spoken words for healing, or use them to cause damage to others. A person's entire view of life can be changed by sincere, well-crafted compliments. Kind words spoken from the heart show people that goodness exists in this world and compassion remains one of the strong bonds among all human beings.

## PRACTICAL WAYS TO SHARE KIND WORDS

- **Be Genuine:** When offering compliments or encouragement, make sure your words are sincere. People can sense authenticity, and genuine kindness has a more profound impact.
- **Be Specific:** Instead of general praise, highlight something unique about the person's efforts or

qualities. For example, "Your presentation was insightful and well-researched" carries more weight than a simple "Good job."

- **Write It Down:** Written words can have a lasting effect. Consider writing a thank-you note, leaving a positive review, or sending an encouraging text message.
- **Practice Active Listening:** Often, kind words stem from truly understanding someone's struggles or achievements. Take the time to listen, and your encouragement will be even more meaningful.
- **Share Publicly:** If appropriate, acknowledge someone's efforts in a public setting, such as during a team meeting or on social media. Public recognition can amplify the positive impact of your words.

## THE RIPPLE EFFECT OF KIND WORDS

Liam's experience demonstrates that genuine encouragement enables people to shift their life path. Individuals who experience defeat or feel invisible can rediscover their self-worth through supportive words, which help them remember their purpose and inspires them to work for their dreams. The process of giving encouragement also leads to increased happiness for the person who offers it.

Speaking positive words helps people develop the fundamental qualities of empathy, gratitude, and self-awareness. Sharing words of kindness creates a chain reaction because people who receive encouragement tend to pass that encouragement along to others through written words, spoken dialogue, and compassionate actions. In addition, positive communication in communities creates trust between people, which enables them to solve problems creatively while connecting with and relying on each other.

## CHAPTER 32

# *Smiles and Hugs*

Maya entered her first day of work feeling nervous and out of her element. The busy office environment intimidated her. Every staff member seemed completely confident, and she doubted her ability to connect with anyone. As she stood in the break room, trying to get her bearings, Tanner, a fellow employee, walked by, gave Maya a warm smile, and let her know he was available if she needed anything.

That brief moment of connection completely transformed her day. Tanner's quick but genuine smile and greeting made her feel seen and gave her the strength to initiate conversations with her new colleagues. Maya eventually developed strong bonds with her coworkers, but she never forgot that first encounter. A month later, she told

Tanner how his friendly gesture had made her feel like she belonged. His smile had provided the encouragement she needed to begin her first day on the job with self-assurance.

Simple gestures like a smile or a hug can have a powerful effect, even though they may seem insignificant. They allow people to connect regardless of background or environment because they transcend all barriers. A smile breaks tension, spreads happiness, and establishes a sense of community. A hug expresses care, empathy, and solidarity in a way that surpasses spoken language. These nonverbal gestures remind people of their shared humanity, especially when the world can make us feel disconnected. Through simple acts, we express value, comfort, and support in direct and meaningful ways.

## THE POWER OF SMILES AND HUGS

People express themselves through hugs and smiles, which can create stronger messages than any verbal communication. A smile enables individuals to establish connections regardless of their cultural origins, age, or present life situation. People experience safety through natural expressions like smiles and hugs, which enables them to build relationships and share positive energy.

And physical expressions such as smiles and hugs are proven to work! Research shows that smiling leads to the release of serotonin and endorphins that promote feelings of well-being, and hugging reduces levels of stress while increasing feelings of security. Given appropriately and with genuine intent, smiles and hugs bring people together and result in deepened authentic relationships.

## PRACTICAL WAYS TO SHARE SMILES AND HUGS

- **Start with Strangers:** A smile can brighten the day of a passerby, cashier, or coworker. Even brief, friendly eye contact paired with a pleasant expression can lift someone's spirits.
- **Offer Hugs When Appropriate:** Pay attention to the needs and comfort levels of others. If someone seems down or overwhelmed, ask, "Do you need a hug?" This simple question can open the door to providing emotional support. (Be prepared to also just share a smile if the person is uncomfortable with hugs.)
- **Be Consistent:** Make it a habit to greet people with a smile and warm demeanor, whether it's

your family, friends, strangers, or colleagues. These small gestures create an environment of positivity and trust.

- **Teach by Example:** Encourage children and others around you to embrace the power of nonverbal kindness. Share stories of how smiles and hugs have impacted you or others.
- **Use Technology Creatively:** While virtual hugs and emojis can't replace the real thing, they can still convey warmth and care in digital spaces.

## THE RIPPLE EFFECT OF SMILES AND HUGS

Maya's first-day-on-the-job nerves were significantly calmed when her coworker Tanner smiled at her. That human connection gave her the confidence to overcome her fears and pushed her to introduce herself to new people.

Sharing warmth with others leads to the giver also experiencing its beneficial effects. Our collective happiness grows when we exchange smiles and hugs. A single smile exchanged between people triggers a chain reaction, which can reshape the surrounding atmosphere and result in stronger communities that are known for their warm and compassionate environments.

CHAPTER 33

# *Helping*

As Mark was heading into his house one day after work, he observed his elderly neighbor, Mr. Jenkins, struggling to carry a load of shopping bags from his car into his home. The heavy bags forced him to stop walking every few steps before he could continue his journey. Concerned about his neighbor, Mark sprinted across the street and offered to assist Mr. Jenkins with his load. Gratefully, he handed some of the bags to Mark and together they chatted about the weather, gardening, and other easy topics as they walked up the driveway. After Mark has finished helping the older man put the bags in the house, Mr. Jenkins expressed, "You have no idea how much this means to me."

The shopping bag delivery task evolved into a

regular occurrence that Mark performed for his neighbor every week. Besides helping carry packages into the house, Mark began visiting with Mr. Jenkins and assisting him with household chores while the two of them chatted. The older man showed his gratitude by telling Mark interesting stories about the past, teaching him valuable life lessons, and even baking him the best chocolate-chip cookies he'd ever tasted.

Mark's simple decision to help Mr. Jenkins carry his groceries into the house became the starting point of a deep and meaningful friendship. What began as a brief act of kindness grew into regular conversations, shared stories, and a sense of mutual care. Over time, Mark found himself checking in with Mr. Jenkins more often, offering help when needed and receiving wisdom and companionship in return. That one small moment of assistance brought unexpected richness to both of their lives, reminding them that genuine connection often begins with the simplest acts of help.

## THE POWER OF HELPING

Mark's life was enriched through the simple act of helping his neighbor with a heavy load. He was rewarded with a sense of purpose and an unexpected new friendship. Mr. Jenkins received help with difficult physical tasks and regular companionship, which kept him from being overwhelmed by loneliness. Both men were grateful for the connection that grew from such a simple moment. Their experience is a reminder that helping others is never a one-sided exchange. When we step in to assist, listen, or support, we often receive just as much in return. Small acts of help create shared moments of dignity, trust, and belonging, strengthening not only individual lives but the communities we are part of as well.

## PRACTICAL WAYS TO HELP

- **Lend a Hand:** Offer to help with physical tasks, such as carrying groceries, mowing a neighbor's lawn, or assembling furniture. These actions show care and create a sense of community.
- **Share Your Skills:** Use your expertise to assist others. Teach a friend how to cook, help a colleague improve their résumé, or tutor a student who's struggling in school.
- **Be Available:** Sometimes, the best help is simply

being present. Offer a listening ear or emotional support to someone who is going through a tough time.

- **Volunteer:** Dedicate time to a cause that matters to you. Whether it's serving meals at a shelter or participating in a neighborhood cleanup, volunteering allows you to make a tangible difference.
- **Start Small:** Even brief moments of help—holding a door open, giving directions, or offering a seat to someone—can have a significant impact on others.

## THE RIPPLE EFFECT OF HELPING

Mark helped Mr. Jenkins with his daily tasks, which brought the older man relief from his daily struggles. Through the act of assisting someone else, Mark experienced increased happiness, which enabled him to create deeper connections in his community. Helping others changes our entire perspective about the world as we develop qualities such as appreciation, self-control, and humility.

The practice of helping also produces a domino effect that travels between different people. People tend to imitate helpful behavior when they witness someone assisting others. This results in stronger community ties while enhancing teamwork and deepening social understanding between people. Small acts of help given consistently help create a world of people who actively help one another.

CHAPTER 34

# *Cheerleading*

JENNA HAD DEDICATED multiple months to preparing a critical presentation at the yearly company conference. She planned to use this presentation to explain her new business concepts to executives before they gave their approval. As the conference drew closer, Jenna started feeling uncertainty and self-doubt. Despite her preparation, she was beginning to question the value of her ideas along with her ability to present them properly.

Tara, a coworker and friend, called Jenna the night before the conference, asking her how she was feeling about the presentation. Jenna answered with complete honesty: "I just don't think I can do this presentation."

Tara responded with complete confidence. "You've worked so hard to get here, and it really shows. Your ideas are great, your skills are solid, and people are going to notice. Everyone in that room will see what you bring to the table. You've gone through so much, and it's only made you stronger. I believe in you—completely."

Tara's encouraging words were still in Jenna's mind as Jenna walked onto the stage the following day. They helped Jenna calm down, and she took a deep breath before starting to speak. When she was done, she was elated to realize the presentation had exceeded her expectations. In fact, she'd received a standing ovation—and there was talk of multiple career advancement paths.

Later, Jenna shared with Tara that her words had provided her with the confidence she'd lacked. That phone call Tara had made, where she'd been a cheerleader for her anxious friend, had turned out to be a transformative moment. For Tara, it had been a quick phone call and a few sincere words of encouragement. But for Jenna, it transported her from self-doubt to confidence.

## THE POWER OF CHEERLEADING

Often, the most important gift we can offer people is our support through encouragement. Every person on earth possesses the ability to be a cheerleader for someone else, to believe in another person's potential and share that belief with them. This takes no financial support or social status—just a genuine commitment to being there for someone else.

Your ability to transform another person's self-doubt into confidence makes you an effective cheerleader. Your declaration of faith in that person enables them to recover their lost inner power. Words of encouragement serve as bright lights during difficult times, guiding people through challenging situations without trying to fix their problems or create flawless solutions. Your emotional support, combined with your belief in another individual, will help them discover their natural abilities and hidden potential. Being a cheerleader for someone else is powerful—you offer unwavering strength and positivity during moments of uncertainty, and you can help change lives.

## PRACTICAL WAYS TO BE A CHEERLEADER

- **Listen Actively:** Sometimes, people need to voice their fears and concerns. Be a sounding board and let them know they are heard and understood.

- **Highlight Strengths:** Remind others of their abilities and past successes. This helps them see their own potential.
- **Celebrate Efforts:** Recognize and celebrate progress, no matter how small. Encouragement isn't just about outcomes; it's about valuing the journey.
- **Offer Perspective:** Help others see challenges as opportunities for growth. Reframe setbacks as stepping stones toward success.
- **Be Consistent:** Make encouragement a regular part of your interactions. A consistent cheerleader provides ongoing support and motivation.

## THE RIPPLE EFFECTS OF CHEERLEADING

Tara's belief in her friend helped Jenna overcome her self-doubts, which allowed her to have a successful presentation and feel confident about her work. The specific encouraging words Tara spoke to her activated Jenna's inner power, and she was able to give her presentation with self-assurance and confidence.

When someone acts as a cheerleader for us, we internalize their positive encouragement, which helps us block out negative thoughts, fear, and anxiety. When we're a cheerleader for others, our optimism and empathy grow stronger as we turn our focus to another person. And positive support travels from one individual to another, creating a community of cheerleaders. Jenna began functioning as a cheerleader for her younger colleagues after she received Tara's support—she wanted to be there for others the same way someone had been there for her.

CHAPTER 35

# *Sharing Knowledge*

NATHAN, A SOFTWARE engineer, had a talent for breaking down complex technical ideas into clear, practical steps others could easily understand. One of his clients was Clara, the owner of a local bakery. When she and Nathan met at a coffee shop to discuss her bakery's financial management issues, she explained how the financial responsibilities at her bakery were creating excessive stress for her because she needed to focus on baking, not finances. She didn't have sufficient time to do both, and she was falling behind on the business end of her job, which was causing her to become extremely anxious.

Nathan offered to help. "I'll show you a simple system that keeps track of all your financial activities. It's easy to use and works in a straightforward way," he explained. Clara expressed doubt about her ability to understand the system, but Nathan assured her she could figure it out. They spent the next few weekends meeting at the coffee shop, going over the system and making sure Clara understood how it worked. Nathan showed Clara how the spreadsheets functioned, demonstrating how to create separate expense and income categories and explaining how she could interpret the data.

After mastering the system, Clara gained greater control over her business operations—and her stress level. Equipped with a better knowledge of her finances and an accounting system that did much of the work for her, Clara was able to increase her bakery profits, expand the business, and make smarter financial decisions. By sharing his knowledge, Nathan had given Clara skills that helped her professionally as well as personally.

## THE POWER OF SHARING KNOWLEDGE

The value of knowledge grows stronger each time we share it, and the act of teaching others helps the teacher expand their own understanding of the subject. Your choice to share your expertise enables others to develop their own abilities, make better decisions, and develop the skills to tackle fresh obstacles and reach peak performance.

You will share knowledge more effectively if you guide people through the learning process. All of us learn better when we're taught self-directed work methods and innovative problem-solving techniques. The transfer of knowledge between people and groups leads to collaboration instead of competition and develops their self-assurance, trust, and understanding. When you share what you know with someone else, you demonstrate that wisdom grows best when it moves freely instead of remaining fixed in one spot.

## PRACTICAL WAYS TO SHARE KNOWLEDGE

- **Teach a Skill:** Whether it's cooking, budgeting, or coding, sharing your expertise can transform someone's life. Offer to teach a friend, family member, or colleague something new.
- **Mentor Someone:** Provide guidance to someone who's just starting out in your field. Share your experiences, insights, and advice to help them navigate challenges.

- **Host a Workshop:** Organize a small class or session to teach a group. This could be anything from gardening tips to career development strategies.
- **Answer Questions:** Be approachable and willing to share what you know when someone asks for help. Sometimes, just a five-minute conversation can provide the clarity and inspiration that's needed.
- **Share Resources:** Recommend books, podcasts, or online courses that have helped you. Pointing someone toward the right tools can be just as valuable as direct teaching.

## THE POWER OF SHARING KNOWLEDGE

Clara received both freedom and self-assurance through Nathan's act of sharing knowledge. A subject that previously seemed impossible to understand was now within her grasp, which made her feel powerful and capable. Her new abilities allowed her to overcome problems, which brought her inner peace. Nathan found purpose through his experience of sharing knowledge with Clara. Teaching enabled him to connect with an individual while building stronger bonds with his community. Once Clara understood her finances, she was able to help another business owner do the same. This is how shared knowledge works. What you teach one person often gets passed on, strengthening others in ways you may never see.

## CHAPTER 36

# *Sharing Experiences*

Laney had always admired people who could cook well. She loved good food, but she doubted her own ability in the kitchen. Most recipes she tried turned out to be a disaster, and she wondered if she'd ever get the hang of culinary skills.

One day, her coworker Dante, an enthusiastic home chef, returned from a weekend food festival, bubbling with excitement. He told her all about the amazing dishes he'd learned to make. Before Dante walked away, he turned to Laney with a smile. "I'm hosting a cooking night at my place this Friday," he said. "You should come."

Laney hesitated. She wasn't sure she'd be any good, and she didn't want to embarrass herself. But Dante assured her it would be fun, relaxed, and beginner-friendly, so she decided to give it a try.

On Friday evening, she arrived at Dante's home and was ushered into the kitchen, where the countertop was neatly arranged with ingredients, fresh herbs, bowls of spices, chopped vegetables, and recipe cards. Dante guided the small group through preparing a simple but delicious homemade pasta dish. Laney learned how to knead dough, simmer sauces, and season food properly while laughing with others about their uneven noodles and flour-covered hands.

As the enticing aroma of pasta filled the kitchen, Laney felt something she hadn't felt in a long time—relaxation. Cooking was actually making her feel grounded and creative. When she finally plated her dish and tasted the result, she felt proud, surprised, and excited. The evening had introduced her to an unexpected sense of accomplishment.

That night created an unexpected shift in her life. Laney started attending weekend cooking classes, trying new recipes at home, and inviting friends to join her for small dinner gatherings. She realized that cooking brought her joy, reduced her stress, and opened a new social circle she'd never imagined being a part of. Through a shared experience, Dante had introduced her to a world she never knew existed and, in doing so, helped her uncover a hidden passion.

## THE POWER OF SHARING EXPERIENCES

Shared experiences with others reveal new possibilities—and often result in new friendships, hobbies, and discoveries. People who participate in shared activities, such as playing sports, cooking, hiking, crafting, or making music, develop self-assurance along with new skills as the process of learning is made natural and fun. And that's not all. When you share experiences with other people, you receive support in confronting your fears or achieving your goals. And that, in turn, serves as inspiration for others to pursue their own individual targets. Connections are created as we encounter identical obstacles while working toward identical aspirations, revealing new strengths and sides of ourselves we may never discover alone.

Sharing meaningful moments with others builds self-confidence, sparks creativity, and strengthens relationships. When people bond while overcoming challenges, trying new activities, or stepping out of their comfort zones, they inspire others to do the same. Shared experiences remind us that we all face similar struggles while striving toward similar dreams.

## PRACTICAL WAYS TO SHARE EXPERIENCES

- **Host an Activity Night:** Invite friends or colleagues to try something new, like a cooking class, a painting session, or a game night. Providing the materials and guidance makes the experience accessible and enjoyable.
- **Take Someone on an Adventure:** Introduce a friend to your favorite hiking trail, museum, or local café. Sharing a place that you love can create lasting memories and inspire new interests.
- **Share a Personal Story:** Open up about a time when you stepped out of your comfort zone or achieved something you never thought possible. Your story might be exactly the encouragement someone else needs.
- **Encourage Participation:** When someone shows interest in an activity, invite them to join you. Whether it's a fitness class, a book club,

or a volunteer event, sharing your passions can inspire others to explore new opportunities.

- **Document the Journey:** Take photos or write about the experience so you can share it with others. Sometimes, seeing a snapshot of someone else's adventure can spark curiosity and motivate others to try it for themselves.

## THE RIPPLE EFFECT OF SHARING EXPERIENCES

A single invitation from a coworker changed Laney's entire outlook on cooking. She began with doubt, stepped into the unfamiliar, and emerged with confidence, joy, and a newfound talent. That experience opened doors to a new hobby, new friendships, and a new way of expressing herself. Dante deepened his passion for cooking by sharing it with others. Helping people discover a new interest brought him genuine happiness and strengthened his relationships. Sharing experiences creates meaningful rewards for both the giver and receiver.

And the positive effects of a shared experience easily and naturally spread outward. Laney eventually began hosting small cooking nights of her own, inviting coworkers, friends, and neighbors to try dishes together.

Her community blossomed into a supportive group that shared recipes, encouraged one another, and celebrated small successes in the kitchen. What started as one invitation evolved into a network of people bonded through food, friendship, and creativity. Shared experiences create strong connections that bring individuals closer and foster communities grounded in encouragement and growth.

SECTION THREE

# NETWORKING NOTHINGS

# *The Doors We Can Open*

Networking is often viewed as a strategic effort—one that requires attending events, cultivating relationships, and making deliberate career moves. While these actions can certainly be effective, networking doesn't always have to be formal or time-consuming. In reality, some of the most impactful connections happen through small, seemingly insignificant actions—what I call "networking nothings."

A networking nothing is any effortless act that helps build relationships, open doors, or support someone's journey—without requiring extensive effort, money, or long-term commitments. It's forwarding a job posting to the right person, introducing two professionals who could benefit from knowing each other, or simply engaging with another individual's social media. These small moments of connection may seem minor, but they can lead to life-changing opportunities.

The beauty of networking "nothings" lies in their accessibility. Anyone, regardless of their industry, experience, or social reach, can practice them. Unlike traditional networking, which can feel transactional or time-intensive, these small acts are natural extensions of everyday interactions. They are about paying attention to the needs of others and taking a moment to help without expecting anything in return.

Think about the times in your own life when a single conversation, recommendation, or referral changed your trajectory. Perhaps someone vouched for you when you weren't in the room, mentioned your name in a meeting, or connected you with a mentor who helped shape your career. More often than not, these moments weren't planned—they happened because someone took a small action on your behalf.

The same principle applies in reverse: You have the ability to create opportunities for others in ways you may not even realize. A quick introduction could lead to a partnership. A positive LinkedIn comment could boost someone's visibility. A casual conversation could spark a new business idea. When you embrace networking "nothings" as a daily practice, you become a bridge for others—helping them reach places they couldn't have accessed alone.

This chapter explores how small, intentional networking gestures—such as offering mentorship, amplifying someone's voice online, or making a warm introduction—can strengthen relationships, foster collaboration, and create opportunities where none seemed to exist before.

Networking is not about what you can *gain* but about what you can *give*. By cultivating the habit of looking for these small moments to connect with and uplift others, you create a culture of generosity and shared success. The more you give, the more your network thrives—and, in turn, the more doors open for you as well.

## CHAPTER 37

# *Mentoring*

EVELYN HAD BEEN retired for nearly three years when she first noticed the young man at the library. It wasn't anything dramatic that drew her attention to him, just the fact that he was always there. Same corner table, same laptop, same posture, slightly folded inward, as if he were trying to make himself smaller. Sometimes she'd arrive before him and leave after him, and in all that time, he never really moved. Week after week, Evelyn watched the same pattern repeat. The young man worked quietly, fingers tapping on his laptop doing his daily work task. Occasionally, he'd lean back in his chair and stare at the ceiling, appearing lost in thought and perhaps a bit frustrated. She knew that feeling all too well. Watching him stirred something in her she hadn't expected. It felt familiar and personal.

One afternoon, as Evelyn packed up her bag to head home, she hesitated. She told herself it wasn't her place. She reasoned that the young man probably didn't want to be bothered. She gave herself a dozen reasons to walk past him like she always did. Then she ignored every one of them. She stopped at his table, smiled gently, and said, "Mind if I ask what you're working on?"

The young man looked up, clearly startled. He paused, as if deciding how honest to be. Then something softened in his expression. "I want to be noticed and challenged more in my job," he said quietly. "But I don't know where to start."

The words came out heavier than he'd probably intended. They carried the weight of years of trying alone. Evelyn didn't rush to fix anything. She simply listened. And when he finished, she said something simple that caught him off guard: "I think you're closer than you realize. It all starts with wanting to do more."

That day didn't end with a plan or a breakthrough. It ended with a conversation. Then another the next month. Then another after that. Soon, the meetings became routine—same table, same coffee, different version of the young man, who Evelyn found out was named Jamar.

They talked about fear, about comparison, and about the quiet voice inside that says, "Maybe this is as far as I go." Evelyn never sugarcoated the process. She told Jamar plainly that growth is slow and rarely fair. But she also told him something else: Lack of recognition is not proof that you are not qualified.

Months passed. Then a year. And without either of them really noticing it, things began to shift. Jamar started raising his hand in meetings. He volunteered for projects instead of waiting to be assigned. He asked questions. Hard ones. He began speaking like someone who expected to be taken seriously. Jamar's promotions didn't come right away. Not even close. But when opportunities finally did appear, he was ready in ways he never could have faked before. When his first leadership role became official, he didn't rush to tell the whole world. He went to the library.

Evelyn was already there when he walked in. She noticed the way Jamar was standing before he even spoke—taller, steadier. He didn't need to explain. She saw it. They just sat there for a moment, coffee between them, both smiling quietly at what steady effort and mentoring can do.

## THE POWER OF MENTORING

Mentorship is the sharing of experience, views, and confidence from one person to another. It's not about control or authority. It's about being present, showing patience, and believing in another person. Mentorship shortens the mentee's learning curve and softens the impact of mistakes and missteps. It also creates a safe place to ask questions, test ideas, and grow without fear of failure. And over time, that steady support is transformed into confidence.

Mentorship replaces doubt with guidance and direction. I have seen the impact of mentorship grow quietly, where a single conversation can shape a decision. That single decision then reshapes a career. And that career eventually touches families, workplaces, and communities.

## PRACTICAL WAYS TO BE A MENTOR

- **Schedule Regular Check-Ins:** Set up consistent time to connect, whether monthly or quarterly, so growth and accountability stay active. These touchpoints create continuity and reinforce that the relationship matters beyond a single moment.

- **Share Lessons from Both Successes and Setbacks:** Be open about what worked and what didn't in your own journey. Sharing mistakes alongside wins gives a realistic perspective and helps others avoid unnecessary discouragement.
- **Set Short-Term, Achievable Goals**: Help break larger ambitions into smaller, manageable steps. Clear goals build momentum and prevent overwhelm while giving a steady sense of progress.
- **Review Résumés, Portfolios, or Presentations Together:** Offer practical feedback on these materials. Fresh eyes can reveal strengths, gaps, and opportunities for refinement that the individual may not see on their own.
- **Practice Interview and Networking Conversations:** Walk through potential scenarios out loud. Practicing responses helps build confidence, improve clarity, and reduce anxiety in real-world situations.
- **Offer Honest, Encouraging Feedback:** Be truthful without being discouraging. Constructive input, when paired with belief in someone's potential, strengthens both skill and confidence.

- **Celebrate Progress, Including Small Wins:** Acknowledge growth at every stage. Small victories build motivation and reinforce that effort—not perfection—is what leads to lasting change.

## THE RIPPLE EFFECT OF MENTORING

Under Evelyn's mentorship, Jamar's confidence grew slowly at first, then steadily. Each small success made his confidence stronger, and that confidence allowed him to speak with assurance in meetings, push ideas forward, and set clear boundaries. What had once felt overwhelming became manageable—and then natural. Emotionally, Jamar felt a shift in his identity. He saw change happening. No longer did he see himself as a person trying to catch up—instead, he was someone who was actively building a future. And he became the leader he'd always wanted to be.

Jamar then became a mentor in his community. Young professionals saw him as an example of inspiration and leadership. His guidance transformed those whom he began to mentor, creating a steady stream of change and impact that went well beyond the two people—Jamar and his mentor, Evelyn—who had started the journey.

## CHAPTER 38

# *Introductions*

Paige had almost skipped the community fundraiser that evening. She'd spent the week moving from one task to the next without stopping to even catch her breath, and now she was feeling the weight of it all. Her feet ached, her inbox was full, and the idea of idle talk over coffee at the fundraiser sounded exhausting. No one was expecting her, no one would miss her, and staying home would have been so easy. But something inside made her grab her jacket and go anyway.

Arriving late, Paige slipped quietly into the back of the room while the crowd settled into the type of small talk she always dreaded. She walked toward the dessert table more out of habit than hunger. As she waited in line, she noticed a man shift awkwardly and glance around as if he wasn't quite sure he belonged there. They exchanged the type of smile that often ends right where it begins, but something inside nudged Paige to say something. They started to chat about the weather, the traffic, the event. Then the man, whose name was Miguel, mentioned that he worked in production and videography. His voice lifted a little when he spoke about his passion for storytelling, but then it softened with doubt as he explained he was trying to get a foot in the door to make this his permanent profession. He had the talent but no connections.

A nonprofit director stood just a few feet away from them. Paige knew the director from work they had done together years earlier. She hadn't seen him for a long time and before she gave it any thought, she opened her mouth and addressed the nonprofit director. "You should meet Miguel," she said, gesturing to her new friend. "He tells stories with his camera. I think you'll like his work."

The director turned and smiled at Miguel. The two of them exchanged small talk, talking a bit about video production and the nonprofit. They exchanged business cards, and then the dessert line moved forward and they went their separate ways. Neither Paige nor Miguel thought much about what just happened. Paige moved on to other conversations before leaving for the evening, and Miguel chatted with a few other people and then headed out.

Weeks later, Paige received a message she hadn't expected. It was from Miguel, and he was writing to let her know he'd been hired to make a documentary. The nonprofit director had remembered him from the dessert table and decided to take a chance. And that wasn't the end of the story. That first project turned into a second project, then a third. Miguel was building a career by doing something he loved.

When the nonprofit held an event to premier the film, Paige was invited to attend. She was impressed by Miguel's work. The story was thoughtful, the pacing was steady, and the images were quietly powerful. After the credits rolled, Miguel spotted Paige in the crowd. He smiled with a confidence she hadn't seen at the community fundraiser. *Sometimes*, Paige thought to herself, *the smallest introduction can change a life.*

## THE POWER OF INTRODUCTIONS

Introductions may feel small, but they often have a big effect: Who gets seen, who gets access, and who gets a real chance at opportunity all depends on who you know.

When one person opens a door for another, trust, respect, and confidence are communicated. The person who has previously been working to make it alone now has an important connection. Introductions create an alignment that might otherwise take years to find. And the power of an introduction is not just in being connected but also in being seen. It encourages people, reinforcing that their work has value—and so do they. A quick introduction has the power to launch careers, give confidence to individuals, and change entire industries.

## PRACTICAL WAYS TO GIVE INTRODUCTIONS

- **Listen for Shared Goals or Complementary Skills:** Pay attention to what people need and what others naturally offer—you'll often spot natural alignment in everyday conversation.
- **Make Warm, Personal Introductions Whenever Possible:** Introduce people directly when you can. Personal introductions feel more authentic and build trust right away.
- **Share a Brief, Positive Context for Both Individuals:** Offer quick insight into who each

person is and why the connection matters, which helps the conversation begin with confidence.

- **Follow Up to Ensure the Connection Was Made:** A simple check-in shows you care about the outcome and helps keep the momentum moving forward.
- **Offer to Host a Short Virtual Introduction If Helpful:** If meeting in person isn't easy, a short video call can quickly break the ice.
- **Encourage Both Parties to Continue the Conversation:** Remind them that the introduction is just the beginning and that the relationship grows through follow-through.

## THE RIPPLE EFFECT OF INTRODUCTIONS

Paige's decision to introduce two people who had something in common had more of an impact than she could have imagined. Given the opportunity to do his first videography project, Miguel gained confidence in his own abilities, and the nonprofit director who hired him discovered a talented individual who could help his organization. The messages Miguel created reached more donors, partners, and volunteers than ever before. Introductions help people grow, open doors that were previously closed, expand networks, and strengthen skills as people work together.

## CHAPTER 39

# *Invitations*

Lila stared at her phone longer than she'd meant to. The text to her running group acquaintance Marcus was already typed out, but she hadn't yet hit Send. They talked occasionally, quick exchanges on group runs, polite small talk at post-run coffee gatherings—but they weren't close. Inviting him to a business expo felt like stepping just beyond the comfortable edge of their connection. Lila worried Marcus might think it was odd. Or worse, that he might feel obligated to come just to be nice. Still, she couldn't shake the feeling that it could make a difference for him.

Lila had been noticing the way Marcus carried himself lately—quiet, a little withdrawn, somewhat preoccupied. More than once, he'd mentioned frustrations about his job search, always with a half-smile that seemed like an attempt to disguise disappointment. But Lila could tell that he was unhappy. And she knew that opportunities like the expo could make a difference. After several minutes of hesitation, she took a breath and sent the invitation.

When Marcus read the message, he set his phone down almost immediately. His first instinct was to decline. Professional settings always made him uncomfortable. He never knew what to say, where to stand, or how to work the room. Too many past attempts had ended with polite smiles and no real leads. But he picked up his phone and reread the message. Lila wasn't pressuring him. She was simply saying she thought the expo might be helpful. And he surprised himself by replying yes.

When Marcus arrived at the business expo, the atmosphere felt overwhelming. Conversations overlapped, laughter echoed, and people moved around the room with confidence. Unsure of where to begin, Marcus drifted toward a quieter booth at the edge of the floor, more out of self-preservation than strategy. But that choice changed everything.

The booth was empty, and the man behind the table

seemed relieved to have someone stop by. What began as a casual conversation turned into an in-depth discussion about skills, experience, and goals. By the end of the exchange, Marcus was offered a formal interview. And just a few days later, the job offer came.

Weeks later, Marcus sent Lila a message: "Thank you for believing I belonged in that room before I believed it myself." And Lila smiled, realizing that sometimes a single invitation is all it takes to change someone's life.

## THE POWER OF INVITATIONS

Invitations open doors, create opportunities for growth, and help people feel like they belong. Many opportunities remain hidden because no one invites people into the room where those chances exist. An invitation allows people to explore possibilities without first proving themselves. It cuts fear by exchanging doubt for access. And an invitation turns a watcher into a doer and a doer, into a contributor. Invitations have the power to build confidence, widen connections, and change how people see themselves. The simple question "Would you like to join me?" can open new paths and completely change the direction of a person's life.

## PRACTICAL WAYS TO OFFER INVITATIONS

- **Invite Without Assuming Interest or Availability:** Extend the invitation without pressure, and let the other person decide what works best for them.
- **Explain Why the Event Might Be Valuable for Them:** Share how it connects to their goals, interests, or current season.
- **Share the Event Details Clearly and Early:** Provide time, location, purpose, and expectations so they feel prepared.
- **Offer to Attend Together if They're Nervous:** Going with someone can ease anxiety and make them feel more confident.
- **Introduce Them to at Least One Person at the Event:** A single connection can make the entire experience feel worthwhile.
- **Follow Up Afterward to See What Stood Out:** A quick check-in helps the other person process the experience and keeps the momentum going.

## THE RIPPLE EFFECT OF INVITATIONS

An invitation can offer far more than access to an event. It can open the door to opportunity, restore confidence, and reintroduce structure and purpose where they may have been missing. For some, a simple invitation leads to connection, employment, or a renewed sense of belonging. What often feels like a small, uncertain gesture to the sender can become a turning point for the person who receives it. Extending an invitation is a way of saying, "You matter," and it has a quiet way of spreading. Those who feel included are more likely to include others, continuing a cycle of connection that grows one invitation at a time.

## CHAPTER 40

# *Referrals*

DURING A MEETING with her boss, Devon was asked if she knew anyone who might be a good candidate for a position that had just opened up in the company. After reviewing the job opening, Trevor's name crossed her mind. They hadn't worked together recently, so Devon hesitated at first. Would Trevor be interested? Was it worth reaching out? Devon reminded herself that referrals weren't promises—they were opportunities. So, she sent the message, trusting that making the connection was enough. As it turned out, the message arrived at the perfect time. Trevor had recently been thinking he needed more professional challenge, and he was excited by the chance to explore a new opportunity.

That single referral changed the tone of everything

that followed. When Trevor was invited to interview, the conversation felt different from the start. The referral gave context. It provided credibility. It signaled that someone inside the organization believed in his abilities. The interview became less about proving worth and more about fit and potential. And when Trevor's job offer arrived, it was clear this wasn't just a position match—it was the result of someone choosing to speak up. The referral didn't guarantee an outcome, but it opened a door that might have remained closed otherwise.

The impact reached beyond employment. Trevor stepped into the role with confidence, knowing someone had been willing to put their name beside his. Devon, in turn, gained a deeper understanding of the influence she carried. Making the referral required little effort, but it created meaningful movement in someone else's life.

Referrals work because they rely on trust, not obligation. They are one of the simplest ways to share opportunity without overextending responsibility. When people choose to recommend, introduce, or vouch for others, they help transform access into possibility. Sometimes, the most powerful thing someone can do is say, "I know someone you should meet."

## THE POWER OF REFERRALS

Referrals are more than recommendations. They provide immediate credibility and reduce the uncertainty decision-makers often face. A referral sends the message that the individual being recommended is worth the effort. For the recipient of the referral, it restores the hope and confidence that rejection may have weakened. Referrals have the power to shape career paths, provide income security, and change a person's self-confidence and outlook on life.

## PRACTICAL WAYS TO GIVE REFERRALS

- **Refer Only When You Genuinely Trust the Person:** Your credibility matters, so only refer people you truly believe in.
- **Highlight Both Skill and Character:** Share not just what they do well, but who they are.
- **Provide a Brief Summary of Why They're a Good Fit:** A short explanation helps others quickly see the value of the connection.
- **Follow Up with Encouragement:** A simple message of support can ease nerves and build confidence.

- **Maintain Integrity with Every Referral You Give:** Each referral reflects your reputation as much as theirs.

## THE RIPPLE EFFECT OF REFERRALS

What began as a single referral extended far beyond a single job opportunity. By choosing to speak up, Devon helped create access that may not have existed otherwise. That one connection reinforced Trevor's confidence, restored his momentum, and reminded him that his skills and experience were valued.

Referrals build cultures of trust within organizations, helping people feel supported rather than isolated. When individuals are willing to recommend others, workplaces become more connected, inclusive, and collaborative. Over time, this practice encourages people to look outward, notice potential in those around them, and help open doors. Referrals also tend to multiply. Those who benefit from being recommended often become advocates themselves, making introductions, sharing openings, or vouching for someone else. In this way, a single referral can quietly influence careers, teams, and communities, proving that meaningful change often begins with just one person who's chosen to make a connection.

## CHAPTER 41

# *Collaborations*

Naomi's notebooks were filled with page after page layered with sketches of playgrounds, shade trees, open community spaces, and wide stretches of grass where children could run freely without fear. She carried her ideas everywhere, tucked into worn journals or on folded pieces of paper in her bag. Every time she passed an empty lot or a neglected park, her mind filled it with color and sound. She could see the vision clearly. What she couldn't figure out was how to make it happen.

Cole, on the other hand, lived in a world of spreadsheets—timelines, budgets, permits, and feasibility reports. Where Naomi dreamed in pictures, Cole dreamed in statistics. And while he could take a vague idea and map it into workable phases, his plans often stayed theoretical.

He knew how to build structure, but not necessarily how to breathe life into it.

Naomi and Cole had crossed paths at a community planning meeting, where both of them had voiced their ideas. Naomi spoke with passion about the importance of creating safe spaces for families. Cole asked practical questions about land use and sustainability. When they chatted with each other after the meeting, they felt like they represented opposite ends of the spectrum.

But when they both joined a planning committee, they realized that maybe their viewpoints weren't as far apart as they'd previously thought. Once that understanding took root, communication followed, and real partnership became possible. Momentum grew. Results multiplied. And Naomi's and Cole's differences actually became a strength as they worked in collaboration to bring about real change in their community's open spaces.

Their partnership wasn't easy at first—it demanded trust. Naomi had to release her grip on every detail and allow someone else to shape the execution of her vision. Cole had to stretch beyond charts and approvals and let real people guide the outcome. At times, they missed each other's vision completely. Other times, they engaged in heated arguments. But slowly, they learned how to listen to and work with each other.

Six months later, the first playground reopened. The gates were unlocked early that morning, and families arrived almost before the ribbon was cut. Children tested the swings with cautious excitement, then abandoned caution altogether. Parents stood nearby, some with tears in their eyes, seeing space that had once felt forgotten coming alive again. Laughter filled air that had been quiet for far too long. Naomi smiled as scenes she'd once only seen inside her notebooks came to life. Cole checked the final inspection report on his phone, then looked up and smiled. What started as hesitant cooperation had become a shared mission—and something amazing was accomplished through positive collaboration.

## THE POWER OF COLLABORATION

Collaboration can turn one person's strength into momentum for an entire group. A single person can help move a project forward, but collaboration accelerates progress. When vision meets execution and ideas stand beside structure, momentum builds and progress happens. Collaboration cuts down on burnout because it's not just one person carrying the load. Skills are combined, relationships are built, trust is established, and communication is increased. Success is no longer measured by one person's actions—it's measured by shared outcomes. And it becomes a model that inspires other groups to work together with a spirit of collaboration.

## PRACTICAL WAYS TO COLLABORATE

- **Identify Complementary Strengths:** Notice where one person's strengths naturally support another's weaknesses.
- **Clearly Define Roles and Expectations:** Clarity prevents confusion and keeps everyone aligned from the start.
- **Set Shared Goals and Timelines:** Clear targets and deadlines give the partnership direction and momentum.
- **Communicate Openly and Consistently:** Regular communication keeps trust strong and issues small.
- **Share Responsibilities and Credit:** Work and recognition should always be distributed fairly.

- **Evaluate Progress Together Regularly:** Checking in allows for adjustments and continued growth.

## THE RIPPLE EFFECT OF COLLABORATION

By sharing responsibility and playing to their strengths, Naomi and Cole grew as leaders together. As each of them became more adaptable and listened to the other person's perspective, they became stronger as a team. Their decision to collaborate resulted in growing trust, and they were able to put aside their differences and find common ground. Because Naomi and Cole chose to work together, families gained a new playground that became a safe, shared gathering place for everyone in the neighborhood. Collaboration strengthens outcomes, builds trust, and shows others what's possible—often inspiring them to step in and contribute as well.

## CHAPTER 42

# *Sharing Resources*

Taylor sent the email to her friend Owen without much thought. It wasn't drafted carefully or reread at all. And it wasn't expertly crafted—it was just a short note, a simple link, and one line typed almost as an afterthought: "This might help." She hit Send and moved on with her day, never guessing how much weight that small message would carry.

Owen opened Taylor's email days later, having returned home after another discouraging day of meetings at work. He sat at his kitchen table, staring at the screen on his laptop for a long time before clicking the link Taylor had sent to an online course she thought he might be interested in taking. The course taught a skill set Owen had always been interested in but never believed he had the time, or courage, to pursue. That night, he told himself he would just look at the first lesson. No commitment. No pressure. Just curiosity.

That one lesson turned into an evening habit.

At first, Owen studied in short, hesitant bursts, unsure of himself and quick to question whether enrolling in this course—and pursuing this career path—was realistic. But as the weeks passed, uncertainty gave way to confidence. Concepts that once felt intimidating started to make sense. His notebook filled up. His questions grew sharper. He wasn't just learning—he was changing.

The evening lessons turned into steady momentum. And somewhere along the way, the version of Owen who was just trying to survive at work transformed into a person who was actively preparing for something more. When Owen completed the online course and began applying for roles in his new field, it felt unreal at first. But each interview strengthened his confidence. And when a job offer arrived, the idea of changing careers didn't feel like taking a sudden leap into the unknown. It felt like stepping onto solid ground that felt familiar.

Later, when Owen thanked Taylor for sending the email, she was surprised. She hadn't imagined it would matter so much. But now she understood that sometimes the smallest act of sharing a resource, sent without fanfare, could become the turning point that makes a difference in someone else's life.

## THE POWER OF SHARING RESOURCES

Sharing resources removes barriers that many people cannot overcome alone, turning limited access into real opportunity and forward movement. Access to information, tools, and learning opportunities can be the difference between moving forward and staying stuck. When resources are shared with intention, progress becomes possible for people, regardless of timing or privilege. Power does not rest in the resource itself, but in how it is offered, explained, and applied. A thoughtfully shared article, tool, or course, paired with context and encouragement, can turn information into action. Over time, this kind of purposeful sharing builds confidence, shapes new paths, and helps individuals and families move toward greater stability and independence.

## PRACTICAL WAYS TO SHARE RESOURCES

- **Share Articles, Tools, or Courses Intentionally:** Send resources with purpose, not just because they're trending.
- **Add a Short Note Explaining Why It's Helpful:** A sentence of context helps the person see the value right away.
- **Encourage Application, Not Just Consumption:** This reinforces that growth comes from using what they learn, not just reading it.
- **Follow Up to See What Was Useful:** A quick check-in shows you care about their progress.
- **Share Both Free and Low-Cost Resources:** Access should never be limited by budget alone.
- **Curate Resources for Specific Goals or Challenges:** Tailoring the resource to the need makes it more powerful.

## THE RIPPLE EFFECT OF SHARING RESOURCES

Sharing resources rarely stops with one person. When someone is given access, clarity, or opportunity at the right moment, the impact often extends far beyond that initial exchange. Confidence grows, momentum builds, and new possibilities emerge, not just for individuals, but for families and communities as well. What begins as a simple article, connection, or tool can move from one person to the next, creating a chain of growth and forward motion. Small acts of sharing, offered with intention, have a way of opening doors we may never see—and with an impact that continues long after the moment has passed.

CHAPTER 43

# *Social Media*

Serena posted her designs quietly, the way she always did. Late at night, after the dishes were done and the house was finally still, she photographed her latest pieces under the soft kitchen light. She adjusted the angles, erased a smudge from the lens, and hesitated over the caption longer than she cared to admit. When she finally hit Post, she didn't wait to see if her post generated any reactions. She'd learned not to expect too much.

Most days, only a few familiar names liked her work—friends who had watched her build this dream from the beginning. The business mattered deeply to her, but it often felt fragile, held together by hope and long hours rather than certainty. She loved creating. She just wasn't sure how long she could keep believing without seeing a way forward.

A friend, Harper, saw Serena's post while scrolling through social media during a short break at work. She recognized Serena's style immediately—clean lines, careful detail, and a quiet confidence woven into every piece. Without really thinking about it, Harper shared the post along with a simple but heartfelt caption describing how much she loved Serena's work. No sales pitch. No flashy claim. Just genuine support.

Serena didn't see Harper's post right away, but the next morning, her phone was going crazy. Notifications kept appearing, new followers, messages, questions about custom orders. At first, she assumed it was a glitch. Then the orders started coming in. One. Then another. Then another. By the end of the day, Serena sat at her kitchen table, stunned—she couldn't believe what was happening. She'd almost been ready to quit, but now anything felt possible.

Over the next weeks, the rhythm of Serena's days changed. She adjusted her schedule, brought in help to package orders, and even upgraded her supplies. Instead of creating with an underlying fear that she was wasting her time and money, she began creating with confidence.

The work felt the same in her hands—but it felt entirely different in her heart.

Later, Serena messaged Harper. She thanked her friend simply and honestly, telling her that couldn't explain how much that one share had meant. Harper was surprised. To her, it had felt like nothing, just a social media share in the middle of a busy day. She hadn't seen the orders being packed late at night, or the smile Serena wore as she carried her first large shipment to the post office. She hadn't seen the way Serena's design business shifted from struggling to viable.

But Serena saw it every day. And long after the initial rush slowed, she never forgot that what carried her forward didn't begin with a marketing plan or a perfect strategy—it began with one person choosing to share her work and say, "This is worth seeing."

## THE POWER OF SOCIAL MEDIA

Social media has the power to transform something that was previously unseen into something of value. You never know what will go viral, and you never know what sharing someone's work might do. Many creators work hard, but without results it can seem like their work doesn't matter.

Yet when that work is shared, it validates what the creator is building. And sharing on social media is effective—it adds reach and credibility, increasing visibility by allowing individual platforms to serve as channels for connection and opportunity.

## PRACTICAL WAYS TO ENGAGE IN SOCIAL MEDIA

- **Share Others' Work Thoughtfully:** Choose posts that genuinely reflect the person's effort and vision.
- **Write Personal, Encouraging Captions:** A few sincere words help the work feel seen and valued.
- **Tag People and Businesses Accurately:** Proper tags help the right audience find the source faster.
- **Comment with Specific Positive Feedback:** Specific encouragement feels more meaningful than generic praise.
- **Share Milestones and Achievements:** Celebrating progress builds momentum and motivation.

- **Support Consistently, Not Just Once:** Ongoing support builds visibility and lasting confidence.

## THE RIPPLE EFFECT OF SOCIAL MEDIA

As Serena's customer base grew, so did her confidence. What once felt discouraging was replaced with motivation fueled by visibility and support. She expanded her product line and began exploring new markets with belief instead of fear. And her customers benefited as well, as they felt good about supporting the work of a local creator. They told their friends, which created a ripple effect in the community of supporting small businesses. Over time, this kind of support became woven into the fabric of the community. When people choose to lift one another up in small, practical ways, growth becomes shared and encouragement turns into lasting momentum.

## CHAPTER 44

# *Letters of Recommendation*

VICTOR DIDN'T WRITE a letter of recommendation for Alina the moment she asked him to. He wasn't hesitant to recommend his intern, but as an attorney, he knew how important the letter would be, and he wanted it to be perfect. As he reflected on their time working together, Victor thought of how Alina would stay late at the office without telling anyone, the calm demeanor she brought into meetings, and the way her colleagues naturally turned toward her when things felt uncertain. These weren't things that would fit on a résumé, but they would work well for a recommendation letter.

Victor did not start the letter by mentioning Alina's titles and accomplishments; instead he started by describing who Alina was when no one was watching. He paused often to reread what he'd written, making sure he was not just describing her performance but also her character. When Victor finished the letter of recommendation, he was proud of what he'd written, satisfied that he'd accurately highlighted Alina's leadership skills and work ethic. Alina read the letter in the car after work. She'd expected support and encouragement but hadn't been prepared to be fully seen. Gratitude overcame her as she read Victor's words—not just for the letter itself, but for the realization that someone truly believed in her.

Weeks later, on an otherwise ordinary afternoon, Alina's acceptance email into law school arrived. She almost missed it. When she opened it, she stared at the words for several minutes before the message really settled in. Then she read it again, just to be sure it was real. This was not an opportunity that was just handed to anyone; it had taken years of effort and dedication.

Victor's letter of recommendation carried Alina's story—and the essence of who she was—to those who eventually sent the acceptance. A story that she could not have delivered herself had made all the difference.

## THE POWER OF LETTERS OF RECOMMENDATION

When you write a letter of recommendation, you speak on behalf of someone else and send the message that this person is worth considering, affirming potential before it is fully visible. Letters of recommendation bridge the gap between capability and opportunity. They also have the power to change established systems by widening the view of who is seen as qualified and worthy. The true power of a letter of recommendation lies in its quiet authority. Well-written words or a confident spoken endorsement often carry more influence than credentials alone.

## PRACTICAL WAYS TO WRITE A LETTER OF RECOMMENDATION

- **Write With Honesty and Clarity:** Clear, truthful language builds trust and credibility with the reader.
- **Include Specific Examples of Impact:** Real moments and outcomes make the recommendation feel genuine and earned.
- **Tailor Each Letter to the Opportunity:** Align the message with what the role, program, or scholarship truly values.

- **Meet Deadlines Without Reminders:** Timeliness shows respect for both the applicant and the process.
- **Offer to Review Before Submission:** A final look can ensure accuracy and confidence in what's being shared.
- **Follow Up with Encouragement:** A simple note of support can steady nerves and reinforce belief.

## THE RIPPLE EFFECT OF LETTERS OF RECOMMENDATION

Alina's acceptance into law school reshaped her direction. Education expanded her professional access and allowed her to set long-term goals with clarity instead of uncertainty. What once felt distant became something she could now actively pursue. Internally, the validation strengthened Alina's self-belief and resilience. Doubt was replaced by confidence rooted in preparation and purpose. Within her field, her presence quietly expanded representation, opening the door for others to see themselves in spaces that once felt unreachable. And in time, Alina would become the one who helped open doors for others.

## CHAPTER 45

# *Brainstorming Sessions*

NATASHA AND DANIEL met for coffee once a week. These meetings weren't rushed—there was no agenda; they simply sat at a table, mugs of coffee in hand, and just talked. The calm of the café made them feel at ease as they spoke. Daniel would arrive with formed ideas, carrying a notebook that held scattered thoughts, unfinished plans, and unanswered questions.

The conversation stayed light at first, concentrating on small talk about work and life. As they sipped their coffee, Daniel eventually admitted that something was weighing on him. He had ideas for a new business but no clear direction. Every option felt tangled, which caused him to fear making the wrong choice, so he wasn't choosing anything.

Natasha listened to Daniel, not rushing or interrupting him. When he was finished, she began to ask questions rapidly, not giving him a chance to think but instead just answer with the first thing that came to mind: "What do you want your work to feel like? What motivates you, and what drains you? What seems too risky to explore?" With each question, the barriers Daniel had built in his mind begin to soften, and he gained a sense of clarity.

After the rapid questions, Natasha and Daniel attacked the hardest question and began to map out some steps, considering every possibility they could think of. They weren't making a detailed plan—they were just using this brainstorming session as a starting point. They discussed setting one reachable goal, taking one small action, having one additional conversation. The point wasn't to have the answers all arrive at once—it was to think about things honestly and with an open mind.

When they left the café, Daniel was equipped with more than notes in the notebook—he now had more direction and the start of a plan.

Soon after the brainstorming session with Natasha, Daniel's once-vague idea turned into the foundation for action. His starting point was hesitation, but deciding to take the first step created a momentum that didn't come from confidence—instead, it came from having clarity about where to begin. He often thought back to that brainstorming session over coffee, realizing that what had changed everything was not specific advice or detailed strategy—it was the act of someone creating space to brainstorm and dream of possibility.

## THE POWER OF BRAINSTORMING SESSIONS

Brainstorming creates space where ideas can exist without immediate pressure to be perfect. It allows possibility to surface before fear has a chance to shut it down. In these shared moments of thinking out loud, uncertainty becomes less intimidating and clarity begins to take shape. What often feels overwhelming in isolation becomes manageable when it's explored with another person. Brainstorming doesn't just generate solutions—it restores courage, reminding people that they're not alone in their questions and doubts. Through thoughtful conversation, half-formed ideas gain structure and hesitation gives way to direction. More than a problem-solving tool, brainstorming can become a catalyst for momentum. It invites movement where there was once paralysis and turns quiet uncertainty into forward motion with purpose.

## PRACTICAL WAYS TO ENGAGE IN A BRAINSTORMING SESSION

- **Offer Uninterrupted Time and Attention:** Be fully present so the person feels heard without distraction.
- **Ask Open-Ended, Thoughtful Questions:** Good questions create clarity instead of pressure.
- **Help Organize Scattered Ideas into Steps:** Turning thoughts into structure makes action feel possible.
- **Provide Neutral Feedback Without Judgment:** Honest, calm input keeps ideas safe to explore.
- **Suggest Next Actions or Experiments:** Small steps reduce overwhelm and build courage.
- **Encourage Forward Momentum:** A gentle push helps prevent clarity from stalling.

## THE RIPPLE EFFECT OF BRAINSTORMING SESSIONS

Daniel's uncertainty gave way to clarity through structured planning, and confidence followed. With direction in place, his actions gained momentum and purpose. The business brought personal stability and renewed meaning to his work. New jobs created opportunities for employees, while the growing services and mentorship outreach strengthened the wider community. What began as a simple brainstorming conversation about a new business idea became a steady current of growth, influence, and purpose.

## CHAPTER 46

# *Small Business Support*

Camille had stopped checking her bank balance more than once a day, not because her financial situation had improved, but because watching the numbers sink lower and lower felt heavier each time. Her small business startup was strong on creativity, loyal customers, and reputation. What it lacked in that season was margin. One slow quarter had quietly turned into two. And fixed costs didn't slow down just because sales had.

Andre first noticed Camille at a local networking breakfast, sitting at a side table with her laptop open but untouched. When he introduced himself and asked how things were going, she gave the answer most small business owners respond with: "Busy. Staying hopeful." But she didn't look hopeful. She looked tired.

Later that week, Andre reached out to his new acquaintance. A community market was coming up—a regional event that drew foot traffic from across three counties. He couldn't promise sales. He couldn't guarantee exposure. But he knew the organizer well, trusted the crowd, and thought Camille's products would resonate with them.

Camille almost declined Andre's offer. Booth fees, prep work, inventory costs—it all felt like one more risk layered onto a season that had already held too many. But something told her this wasn't about pushing through fear. It was about choosing visibility over retreat. And so she said yes.

On the weekend of the market, the weather was poor and expectations were low. Camille arrived early, set her booth up quietly, and told herself the win was simply in showing up. But by midmorning, people started stopping to see Camille's work. Asking questions. Touching the materials. Telling her they hadn't seen anything like this before. Much to her surprise, by early afternoon, she had sold nearly half her inventory.

But the real shift came in what followed.

Two shop owners placed wholesale orders. A

regional buyer asked about seasonal lines. And the following week, several new customers found Camille online after recognizing her brand from the market. For the first time in months, cash flow stabilized naturally, not through rescue, but through momentum. Camille didn't rebuild her business overnight. But she rebuilt steadily. Thoughtfully. With confidence instead of panic.

When she thanked Andre, he reminded her gently, "All I did was invite you into the room. You built everything else." And Camille realized that sometimes support doesn't arrive as a solution—sometimes it arrives as a door that allows effort to finally breathe.

## THE POWER OF SMALL BUSINESS SUPPORT

Supporting small businesses is not a money exchange; it actually communicates trust in a person's dream while supporting their efforts and courage. Every purchase, every referral, every introduction, tells a small business owner that their work matters and the risk they are taking is noticed. Small businesses are often built in seasons of uncertainty, fueled by resilience rather than security. When support shows up at the right moment, it creates breathing room where fear once lived, and it's then that small businesses can switch from survival mode to growth mode. Often, a small business's success will reach beyond the business owner, as that business then supports local families, employees, and communities. Local economies grow steadier. Relationships deepen. Purpose expands. What looks like a simple decision to support a small business often becomes much more than that, strengthening the greater community.

## PRACTICAL WAYS TO SUPPORT A SMALL BUSINESS

- **Share Vendor Recommendations Publicly:** Public recommendations build both visibility and trust.
- **Make Warm Client Introductions:** Personal introductions create stronger connections than cold outreach.
- **Leave Reviews and Testimonials:** Actual experiences reassure future customers and strengthen credibility.
- **Promote Launches and Milestones:** Celebrating key moments boosts momentum and morale.

- **Refer Consistently, Not Just Once:** Ongoing referrals create sustainability, not just spikes.
- **Offer Feedback and Encouragement:** Support behind the scenes builds confidence for the long haul.

## THE RIPPLE EFFECT OF SMALL BUSINESS SUPPORT

When Camille decided to say yes to a business-expanding opportunity, that decision restored her cash flow—and, more importantly, her confidence. The first weekend of sales started the momentum. And then Camille built the momentum with purpose, not panic, and the momentum kept growing steadily. The impact reached beyond her business. New orders benefited suppliers and vendors. Customers became key players in rebuilding her business. What began as a simple invitation turned into a shared effort, reminding the community that small businesses grow strongest when they are lifted together. As stability returned, so did dependable income for families, and the business took root as a lasting part of the community.

## CHAPTER 47

# *Alumni Networks*

Tyler had always been the type of person who handled things quietly. Even when the diagnosis he'd been dreading came, he tried to manage the appointments, the medication schedule, and the rising medical bills on his own. He didn't want to burden anyone, least of all the people who remembered him only from school days and scattered reunions. He told himself he would figure it out. He always had.

Tori heard about Tyler's situation through a mutual friend. They hadn't been especially close back in college, but she remembered Tyler as steady, humble, and always kind. Something about the news of his diagnosis stayed with her long after the conversation ended. That evening, she opened her university's alumni network social media page, hesitated briefly, then typed out a message asking if anyone within their community could help, whether through resources, advice, or simply showing up for someone who had once shown up for them. She hit Post and hoped her message might reach a few people.

It reached more than a few.

Within hours, messages began pouring in. Former classmates asked for details about Tyler's situation. A retired nurse offered guidance. A social worker shared information about financial support programs. Someone who barely remembered Tyler started a small fundraiser, expecting only modest participation. By the end of the week, the fundraiser had grown far beyond what anyone planned. Alumni donated in small amounts, then larger ones. Comments filled with memories, encouragement, and fond stories about Tyler. What had once felt like an isolating struggle began to feel like shared humanity.

Tyler was overwhelmed when Tori told him what she'd done. He didn't know whether to cry or protest. But as the support continued to arrive—ranging from rides to appointments to meal deliveries to someone even covering a month of medication—gratitude and acceptance slowly replaced shame and embarrassment. The help didn't fix everything, but it lifted enough weight for Tyler to breathe again. And in the quiet spaces between appointments, he realized something he hadn't allowed himself to feel in a long time: He wasn't alone.

Tori never imagined her message would ripple so far. To her, it had been a small ask. To Tyler, it felt like being carried. And to the alumni community, it became a reminder that connection doesn't end when school does—it just waits for moments that bring it back to the present.

## THE POWER OF ALUMNI NETWORKS

Alumni networks offer more than shared history. They connect people through common experiences, seasons of life, and formative memories. While these networks often support career growth, their deeper value lies in belonging. Members know they are not navigating life alone. When one person speaks up about a need or opportunity, those shared memories become a reason to act. What once connected people in the past can move them to create change in the present. In this way, individual challenges can become collective efforts, and long-standing connections can turn into meaningful support. Alumni networks show that community grows over time, strengthened by shared history and renewed when someone chooses to reach out and reconnect.

## PRACTICAL WAYS TO UTILIZE ALUMNI NETWORKS

- **Reach Out on Behalf of Someone in Need:** A single message can activate support faster than one person ever could alone.
- **Share Fundraisers, Medical Needs, or Crisis Support:** Timely sharing allows the community to respond with care and resources.
- **Leverage Shared History to Build Trust Quickly:** Common experiences create instant credibility and connection.
- **Coordinate Support Beyond Financial Giving:** Meals, transportation, childcare, and encouragement matter just as much as money.
- **Reconnect People Who Have Lost Touch:** Life pulls people apart—but shared roots can still bring them back together.
- **Follow Up with Gratitude and Updates:** Closure strengthens the bond and reminds the community that their support mattered.

## THE RIPPLE EFFECT OF ALUMNI NETWORKS

The alumni-network support system that Tori began for Tyler brought back his dignity, gave him a measure of peace, and reestablished connections from the past during his time of uncertainty. The financial assistance he received brought short-term relief, yet the true value emerged from his realization that people remembered him, cared for him, and wanted to support him. Tori's initial message triggered a sense of camaraderie among the alumni members as they came together to help Tyler, showing compassion in a way that erased the distance between them.

When people choose to engage, shared history turns into meaningful support. A single message can activate a network that is already connected, transforming passive membership into real belonging and action.

## CHAPTER 48

# *Skill Swaps*

Faith met Lucas through a friend at a community gathering that neither Faith nor Lucas had planned to attend. Their first conversation wasn't particularly memorable—just small talk about work, the community, and the event they were attending. But after they discovered they had some common ground, they scheduled a follow-up meeting for a few weeks later. And it was at their second meeting that Faith and Lucas each saw a need that the other person could meet.

Faith had built a service business with skill and determination, but she was feeling overwhelmed by the marketing and online organizational components of the business such as Google Drive. Lucas, on the other hand, was naturally gifted at design and online systems. And he struggled where Faith excelled—managing budgets, determining pricing, and creating a basic business structure.

After their conversation, Faith and Lucas decided to help each other by exchanging skills, based on set expectations and mutual respect. Faith helped Lucas organize his pricing, contracts, and financial workflow. In return, Lucas rebuilt Faith's website, improved her brand image, and streamlined the systems that had been slowing her down. There were no vague promises made—only agreed timelines, honest feedback, and steady communication.

What started as a short-term solution slowly grew into a steady partnership as they learned to rely on each other and share responsibilities. Faith no longer felt held back by spending too much time on the tasks that she hated and struggled with. Lucas no longer felt overwhelmed by the financial aspects of his job while trying to manage the design and online work. Each of their businesses became stronger because they no longer had to do everything alone—they had someone to help them with the hard parts.

What had begun as a simple exchange of skills became long-term stability for both Faith and Lucas. By engaging in a skill swap, they were able to move their businesses forward. And they recognized that what felt like nothing to one individual was exactly what the other needed most.

## THE POWER OF SKILL SWAPS

Skill swapping turns limitation into forward movement. We don't have to be good at everything in order to grow at something. When two people share what comes naturally to each of them, both move ahead without the weight of trying to carry it all alone. Skill swapping replaces isolation with partnership and transforms frustration into progress. It also restores respect. Each person gives and receives with equal value, removing the imbalance that often comes with traditional help. What feels like nothing to one person becomes everything to another. These exchanges have the power to build confidence, create stability, restore dignity, and produce lasting growth.

## PRACTICAL WAYS TO SWAP SKILLS

- **Clearly Define the Skills Being Exchanged:** Clarity prevents confusion and sets fair expectations from the start.

- **Set Boundaries and Timelines:** Boundaries protect the relationship and keep the exchange balanced.
- **Match Effort and Value Fairly:** Both sides should feel equally respected and invested.
- **Document Agreements if Needed:** A simple outline helps prevent misunderstandings later.
- **Review Results Together:** Constantly check strengths, weakness, outcomes, and threats (SWOT).
- **Celebrate Mutual Success Openly:** Shared wins reinforce trust and long-term partnership.

## THE RIPPLE EFFECT OF SKILL SWAPS

Faith and Lucas felt immediate relief through their shared support. Tasks that had once felt overwhelming became manageable, and the pressure of trying to do everything alone began to lift. Their exchange reminded them that support doesn't always arrive as rescue—sometimes it shows up as shared strength.

Over time, skill swapping grew into stability for each of their businesses. Improved operations brought clearer systems, steadier income, and stronger confidence in decision-making. What had once felt reactive became intentional. Each of them gained the freedom to focus more fully on the work they did best. And the impact reached beyond just the two of them. As their services improved, clients experienced greater consistency, quality, and reliability. The skill swap eventually grew into a model others began to follow. Collaboration works when it's built on clarity and trust—and it has the ability to reach far beyond the original partnership.

## YOUR "NOTHING" CAN CHANGE THE WORLD

Networking "nothings" demonstrate that even the smallest gestures can have far-reaching impact. Whether it's mentoring someone, extending an invitation, leveraging technology, or acting as a conduit, small acts of generosity create a web of support that empowers individuals and strengthens communities.

When you offer mentorship, you're not just guiding someone; you're planting seeds of confidence and growth that can flourish into a forest of opportunities. An invitation to a simple event could open the door to life-changing connections, just as a single introduction might inspire a new partnership or career. Technology amplifies these possibilities, offering a platform where boundaries dissolve and opportunities multiply.

Being an active conduit means recognizing the unique strengths of others and facilitating connections that allow those strengths to shine. It's about seeing potential where others might not and using your "nothing"—your time, your connections, your encouragement—to help others realize their dreams.

These actions create a ripple effect. When one life is uplifted, it often inspires that person to uplift others. A mentor nurtures a future mentor. A kind word today becomes the foundation for someone's bold decision tomorrow. A shared resource can cascade through communities, touching countless lives.

It's important to remember that you don't need extraordinary resources or influence to make an impact. The true power lies in intention. By sharing what you have, no matter how small it may seem, you contribute to a cycle of generosity and empowerment that can transform lives and strengthen communities.

So, the next time you feel you have nothing to give, think again. Your "nothing" might be exactly what someone else needs to take the next step, overcome a challenge, or realize their potential. Together, through these seemingly small acts of generosity, we weave a network of support, collaboration, and growth that has the power to change the world.

CONCLUSION

# *Turning Small Acts into Lifelong Impact*

THE CONCEPT OF "nothing" is a powerful reminder that even the smallest gestures can create a lasting impact. Whether through financial support, time, or networking, every action has the potential to shape someone's future. By embracing this mindset, we shift our perspective from focusing on what we lack to recognizing the abundance of opportunities we have to make a difference. Here are some simple yet meaningful steps you can take:

### *Financial "Nothings" Action Items*

- **Support Local Charities:** Identify a cause you care about and commit to making small, consistent donations.

- **Tip Generously:** The next time you dine out or order coffee, leave a little extra for someone who depends on those tips.
- **Sponsor a Student or Family:** Even a small scholarship fund or a contribution to a family in need can have a ripple effect on their future.
- **Create a Giving Jar:** Set aside spare change or a small portion of your earnings each month to donate to a meaningful cause.
- **Encourage Collective Giving:** Get friends or colleagues to pool small donations for a bigger impact.

***Time "Nothings" Action Items***

- **Volunteer Regularly:** Find a nonprofit or community organization where you can donate your time on a weekly or monthly basis.
- **Be Present for Others:** Make an intentional effort to check in on friends, family, or coworkers who may be going through a tough time.

- **Offer Mentorship:** Share your knowledge and experience with someone looking for guidance in their personal or professional life.
- **Practice Active Listening:** The next time someone confides in you, put aside distractions and give them your full attention.
- **Perform Small Acts of Kindness Daily:** Hold the door open, help a neighbor with a task, or write a note of encouragement to someone who needs it.

### *Networking "Nothings" Action Items*

- **Make Meaningful Introductions:** Connect people in your network who might benefit from knowing each other.
- **Share Opportunities:** If you come across a job posting, grant, or scholarship, pass it along to someone who might need it.
- **Promote Others:** Support small businesses, freelancers, or nonprofit initiatives by sharing their work with your social network.

- **Offer Guidance:** If someone is looking for career advice, share your insights or connect them with someone who can help.
- **Champion Others' Success:** Celebrate the achievements of those around you, whether publicly or privately, to encourage and uplift them.

The beauty of giving our "nothing" is that it often leads to something far greater than we could ever imagine. When we contribute in small ways, we build a culture of generosity that inspires others to do the same. The impact of a simple act of kindness can extend far beyond the moment—it has the ability to create a chain reaction of goodwill that transforms lives and strengthens communities.

Every day presents new opportunities to give, even in the smallest of ways. By remaining mindful of financial, time, and networking "nothings," we step into a life of purpose, connection, and collective support. The world needs what each of us has to offer, so take the first step and see how even your smallest action can make the biggest difference.

What type of "nothing" can you give today?

# *Acknowledgments*

I AM DEEPLY GRATEFUL to **Andy Andrews** for his guidance, training, and encouragement along this journey. His wisdom, perspective, and commitment to purposeful living have influenced not only this work, but the way I approach impact, leadership, and service. I am thankful for the lessons learned and the inspiration to look beyond the obvious and act with intention.

I also wish to honor the memory of **Alice Whitaker** (May 6, 1939—April 13, 2025), who I dearly wish could have seen this book completed. She helped me understand, long before these pages existed, that nothing truly can be everything. She was there when I first coined the phrase *My Nothing Is Someone Else's Everything*, and her presence, wisdom, and belief in small acts with great meaning live on through this message.

I would also like to extend my sincere thanks to the publisher, editorial, and full release team at **Forefront Books** for their professionalism, expertise, and support in bringing this book to life. Their guidance through the editing, production, and release process helped shape this message and ensured it reached the reader with clarity and care.

I would like to extend my heartfelt thanks to **Kiaunna** for her steadfast support throughout this process. Her help in keeping me on schedule, working through website details, and providing consistent encouragement made a meaningful difference in bringing this book to completion.

I also extend my sincere appreciation to the **IAITAM staff** for their patience, support, and willingness to help while this book took shape. Their understanding, flexibility, and quiet encouragement made space for this project to be completed, and I am truly thankful for each of them.

Finally, to my husband **David**—thank you for standing beside me with unwavering support, even when my "nothing" takes the form of wildly ambitious ideas. To **Ashlyn** for constant proofing and keeping me on track. To all **my children, family, and friends**, you are the constant encouragement behind every step forward. Your love steadies me, your patience sustains me, and your belief makes the journey possible. I love you all.

# *About the Author*

Dr. Barbara Rembiesa (Dr. Barb) is the founder, CEO, and president of the **International Association of IT Asset Managers (IAITAM)**—the world's leading authority on IT Asset Management education, certification, and professional standards. Under her leadership, IAITAM has empowered thousands of organizations in over 120 countries to manage technology assets responsibly, reduce risk, and maximize business value.

A respected strategist and entrepreneur, Dr. Barb's career began in the financial and consulting sectors, where she led enterprise-level technology tracking projects, negotiated complex software compliance resolutions, and designed disaster recovery frameworks for some of the nation's most prominent institutions. Her deep industry experience laid the foundation for IAITAM's mission: to professionalize IT Asset Management and establish it as a critical business discipline worldwide.

Beyond her executive leadership, Dr. Barb is an **acclaimed author and speaker**, inspiring professionals to lead with integrity, vision, and service.

With more than twenty-five years of leadership, innovation, and advocacy, Dr. Rembiesa continues to shape the intersection of **technology, governance, and humanity**, ensuring that IAITAM and its global community remain at the forefront of responsible digital management and positive change.